TURN RIGHT AT THE
NEXT CORNER

To
Sue —
Good Luck —

Keep turning right!,

Pat Vir
6-15-92

TURN RIGHT AT THE NEXT CORNER

PAT VIVO

Trudy Knox, Publisher
Granville, Ohio

Trudy Knox—Publisher
168 Wildwood Drive
Granville, OH 43023-1073

First Edition
Sue Politella, Editor

ISBN: 0-9611354-3-3
LCN: 91-090225

To my parents
Mary Mamula Gilboy and Leo Ray Gilboy
whose memories warm me daily.
They brought me forth, loved and nourished me.
All that I am, I owe to them.

CONTENTS

PREFACE

As a professional public speaker I talk to both teen-age and adult groups all over the country. My most popular speech has been "Turn Right at the Next Corner," which deals with the decisions we make.

One day not long after I had spoken to a high school assembly I got a letter from a girl who had been there.

"I have 46 pills in front of me that I'm going to take after I finish writing to you," she began, "and after you hear the kind of life I've had you'll know why I have decided to do away with it."

For page after page she described a life of abuse and the indifference of people around her. As I read it I became physically ill from feeling her pain.

After she told her story she ended by saying, "Mrs. Vivo, I feel so much better after talking to you and just pouring my heart out that I am going to flush these pills down the toilet, because I can still make something of my life. You had a lot of terrible things happen to you, and you still made something of your life."

The things that happened to me were very different from her experiences, but from childhood until my late teens I knew what it was to feel like an outsider. Even though there were fun times, there was always that underlying feeling that I didn't really fit in with the others.

Because I experienced rejection and still managed to survive I've been able to relate to many young people who have felt that same pain.

This is the story of how it all happened.

ACKNOWLEDGMENTS

I would like to express my appreciation to the following people who helped bring this book to life:

My sisters and brother, Lee Ohrt, Dot Creps and Leo Gilboy who helped reconstruct childhood memories, whose moral support was unending, and whose love was always felt.

My husband, Tony, who allowed me the freedom and creativity to be what I am and encouraged my endeavors. He will always be remembered as a good husband, a caring father, a superb grandfather and a popular politician.

My children, Janis, Anthony, Allison, Alicia, Allan, Angela, Andrew and Andrea, who are so special to me that there are no words adequate to express my love for them. They are my life and I shall cherish them forever.

Barbara Yoder Hall, who inspired me to write this book and molded its direction and content. I shall never forget her.

and

To all the young adults in my life whose troubles seem so big they cannot be solved: remember that there are so many tomorrows waiting for you.

I.
Growing Up

As the oldest child of deaf parents my background was different from that of most people. Being different meant that I didn't really fit in with other children when I was small. That hurt. But there were wonderful times too, and today I am grateful for all of my experiences, even the painful ones, because they made me who I am.

Mother and Dad

My parents lost their hearing from childhood diseases, and it was a hard struggle to overcome their handicaps. Even harder was falling in love with each other, which brought some stormy years because neither family approved of the other. Dad was a redheaded Irishman from a devout Catholic family, while Mother was Greek Orthodox and Serbian.

In the eyes of both families this romance was bad news. Each resented that their child was going with a foreigner, and worse yet, someone from another religion. There was so much resistance that it was seven years before they could get married. Mother, Mary Mamula, was born in Pittsburgh on September 16th,

1901, the third of seven children. Later they moved to Mingo Junction, Ohio, where there was a large Serbian community. Her parents were hard-working blue collar people. Her father worked in the steel mill and her mother stayed home and raised her family. All of my grandparents died before I was born.

When she was three-and-a-half, Mother came down with scarlet fever and lost her hearing. When she was five my grandmother sent her to the Ohio School for the Deaf in Columbus. She loved it and stayed there for twelve years, going home only for Christmas and summers.

Her education emphasized the basic homemaking skills necessary for survival: cooking, sewing, knitting, crocheting. In those days they did not consider grammar that important and it took a back seat. Mother never was very good at it.

She was basically a happy person and she never saw herself as handicapped. Instead she felt sorry for those poor blind people.

Father, Leo Ray Gilboy, was 100% Irish, with a Flannery for his mother. He was born in Youngstown, Ohio, on February 6th, 1896, and he became deaf from spinal meningitis, which he caught at the age of four.

His family sent him to St. Mary's, a private Catholic school for the deaf. Unlike Mother, he was not very grateful for the opportunity, and he tried to run away several times. For the first couple of years he would cry when his parents took him to the train.

When he finally got used to the school he loved it. They had an excellent athletic program there and he was active in baseball, basketball and other sports. His school also required that they learn written language skills, and he had a wonderful command of

English. He was extremely bright and interested in everything. He enjoyed a broad range of reading, even encyclopedias, and he especially loved the *National Geographic*. He would pore over every page of it with great pleasure. He was interested in science, and if they'd had the right kind of training for deaf people in those days he might have become a doctor.

St. Mary's also offered vocational training and he chose to learn the printing trade. He was an accomplished printer and readily found work in Youngstown.

There was an annual Tri-State picnic for the deaf with people from Ohio, Pennsylvania and West Virginia. Mother and Dad met there and liked each other right away, but the ethnic and religious differences were too much for their families. When Dad was courting Mom he even went to the back door so as not to disturb them too much with a front door entrance.

The long engagement gave Father time to save enough money to build a house in Boardman, a Youngstown suburb. He was a good do-it-yourselfer, but not for anything that big, so he had the work done.

Their parents must have finally decided to accept the inevitable, and they were married in a Catholic church in Youngstown. Although Mother didn't convert then, she agreed to raise the children as Catholics, and eventually she converted to Catholicism.

After they were married and waiting for the house to be completed, they lived in his old family home with his unmarried brothers and sisters. His parents were both dead by that time.

At first his family wasn't too happy with Mother because they were still concerned with the religious differences, but learned to love her during the months they all lived together. She was so warm and sunny that they couldn't help it, and they soon realized she would make a wonderful wife for Dad. Living with in-laws was still difficult, however, and Mother was glad to move into her own home.

Their marriage was smooth because Father was The Boss and Mother accepted it. He made all the decisions, while she acquiesced and was the "perfect wife." She was a saint! She never crossed him or talked back.

Father was not easy to live with. He was loving, but also stern and demanding. Mother was more concerned with a clean house than finding time to play, walk, or swing with the children. Her days were filled with cleaning, washing, ironing, sewing, crocheting, knitting and cooking. Yet for all of her busyness I was closer to her than to Father.

Mother was pretty, pleasantly plump, and had an olive skin from her Serbian heritage. Her efficiency and time management would have made her the envy of today's executives. She had a schedule and followed it closely. She washed the clothes on Monday and ironed them on Tuesday. Her ironing always included quantities of shirts because Dad wore a fresh one every day. On Wednesday she did odd jobs, such as cleaning the windows. Thursday she changed and washed all the linens, and Friday she cleaned the entire house, including moving the furniture, dusting, waxing, and doing whatever else was necessary to keep everything in tip-top condition. Saturday she scrubbed the kitchen floor. When she finished early or otherwise had spare time she scrubbed the front porch.

She even found time to do some ironing for Aunt Katharine, who was the career woman in Dad's family. She had gorgeous clothes, loaded with ruffles and pleats, and I remember Mother painstakingly doing all of it. I don't know what Aunt Katharine paid her, but I'm sure it was minimal. Still, Mother was glad for the extra income.

Every nice morning Mom would put on little slip-on rubbers or galoshes and go outside to cut flowers, check her plants, or put up the clothesline if Dad hadn't done it earlier. She was meticulous about the rubbers because she didn't want to get her feet wet from the morning dew.

Mother was a hard worker but I don't really think you'd call her a workaholic. She knew how to relax and she enjoyed television if it was animated, and she liked playing cards with her deaf friends. She also found it relaxing to crochet, and she made beautiful tablecloths and dresser scarves.

She also wanted to look nice, and every Friday like clockwork she plucked her eyebrows, using a magnifying mirror to make sure she did a thorough job of it. Though her clothing was simple, she always looked attractive.

She never learned to drive. Dad took her places when he could, but if she wanted to go downtown shopping during the day when he was working, she took the bus or trolley. She preferred the smoother bus ride, finding the trolley too bumpy and swaying. She usually went to McKelvey's Department Store to buy whatever clothes she didn't make for us.

She baked fabulous pies, and in later years when she sometimes bought frozen pies hers still turned out better than ours did. She was a good cook and could do great things with leftovers, but she cooked for Dad rather than the rest of us. He was a meat-and-potatoes man who wanted his meat loaf well done and dry.

Father had ruddy skin and was very healthy and good looking. He was slim and medium tall, about 5'11". He had a brisk jaunty walk, and his intense blue eyes took in everything immediately. He had a tremendous sense of humor and could find something funny in most things, but when he was on a serious subject he did not want to be sidetracked.

He was strongly self-disciplined and responsible, and he poured himself into everything he did. He worked at the United Printing Company for 46 years, and in all that time he missed only three days from work. They loved him. Since he was deaf he didn't lose any time talking, but just stayed at his machine all day.

He had trained himself to wake up naturally in the morning since he'd never have heard an alarm. He never took a lunch to work, but at noon he'd stop at a nearby restaurant for a cup of coffee and a piece of pie. He had a sweet tooth and loved dessert. He had a big supper when he got home, with more dessert, of course. Mother baked every day to satisfy that tooth. She often made rich, gooey cinnamon breakfast rolls from scratch, except that we never had them at breakfast. They were strictly dessert and served at supper.

Dad always helped Mom with the dishes, and he often put up the clothesline on wash day. He did all of the house maintenance jobs and became quite skilled with tools, taking great pride in using them effectively.

He developed a number of habits to compensate for his deafness. For instance, every night in the middle of the night he got up and made the rounds of the house, checking to see that the doors were locked, the water and the stove were off, and the windows closed. It was a way of insuring that every-thing was safe, since he couldn't have heard in-truders, a stove explosion or plumbing problems.

Because he was so disciplined he wanted us to be the same way, and we were all scared of him. Some-times you could get around Mother, but you couldn't cross the line with Dad. When we were ornery he would make horrible guttural sounds which served as a warning. When we were really bad he would take out his razor strap or belt and smack us across the buttocks. The punishment came immediately when we misbehaved, and five minutes later it was over. Although he had a temper he got over it quickly and never held old grudges. We all knew we were loved.

There was no question that Dad ran our home—you just felt his presence there. Mother reinforced this by deferring to him in almost everything: "Ask your Dad." "See what Dad says." "If it's all right with your Dad, you may do it."

Mother had a more easy-going personality and I used to take advantage of her. If I wanted to go some place I'd make up a couple of extra reasons so Mom would let me go, and she in turn would talk Dad into it. If I went to him first he would sometimes say no, and that was that.

There were other times when I took advantage of her deafness. If I had a phone conversation and didn't want to take the time to explain to her what it was all about, I'd make up something to tell her when she asked about it. Later when I was in college and dating Tony Vivo, if we had an argument over the phone I'd lie about that. I wanted her to like him, and I wanted him to look good to her.

In later years when television came out Mother

and Dad both enjoyed it, though not the same programs. They were usually able to follow the action in spite of their deafness. Dad loved to watch the Dracula shows and the mysteries, and he insisted that the bad guy always had the mustache. He was right!—in those days the bad guy did. Mother preferred the game shows, and she would have loved "Wheel of Fortune" today. She liked highly animated slapstick comedies such as "I Love Lucy." The newscasts and other dialogue-type programs were boring to both of them.

Over the years Dad owned several makes of cars. He drove a Terraplane, then a Hudson and later a DeSoto. We couldn't remember all the varieties, except that for some reason he disliked Fords and would never own one.

Childhood

Until I was three I don't ever remember hearing the spoken word, but I knew sign language for Mother, Father, love, dog, house, cookie—enough for my needs.

That year Mother started sending me to Aunt Annie's a few days at a time when it was convenient. Aunt Annie was the wife of Dad's brother Martin. She had fourteen children, including several sets of twins, so one more little one didn't make that much difference. There I learned what it was like to live in the world of the hearing, and Aunt Annie was a close and valuable ally.

When I was four-and-a-half Dad bought me a radio and I continued my explorations in the world of sound. Even so, one problem which came from not hearing speech from the beginning was that I had a speech defect: I stuttered. Of course, my parents weren't aware of this so they couldn't take steps to help me overcome it, and the problem plagued me all the way through high school.

Before I went to school I didn't realize that I was different, since home was a loving place where I was totally accepted. All that changed when I got on the school bus for the first time and met the outside world. The other children made fun of me and of my parents.

"Here comes Patty," they said. "She's got those dummy parents who wave their hands around like idiots." They imitated my parents' guttural sounds all the way to school and all the way back home. Every day they had some fun at my expense and every night I cried myself to sleep. I'd ask, "God, why did you give me a mother and dad that other children laugh at? Why couldn't I have normal parents? Why couldn't I have Sally's or Betty's parents? They're normal and you can understand them when they talk."

Sometimes I was the butt of their jokes because of my stuttering, and they'd imitate my halting speech. This left me extremely self-conscious when I had to speak in school. When we had oral recitation scheduled or when we'd go around the room and read a paragraph I'd die inside. I'd wonder what paragraph I'd have to read, and I half prayed and half thought, I hope the bell rings before she gets to me. Fear would sweep over me as I questioned whether there'd be words I'd stumble over, and there was a terrible gut feeling that it would be a disaster. Whenever I had to do reports in front of the class I felt weak all over. Even after I sat down again I worried about how badly I must have done.

When I first started school I had a difficult time with language because I tried to translate signing literally. It got me into grammatical trouble, and the teachers emphasized that it was not "Me go to bathroom," but "I want to go to the bathroom."

Because of these experiences I was always afraid that I was probably wrong. Once in the first grade I was told to bring a "proverb" back to school. I was in a panic. What on earth was a proverb? I somehow signed the word for my parents. My father found the dictionary and in it an example: "A sleeping cat catches no rats."

I was sick, certain that he had made a mistake, because the sentence made no sense. How could that be a proverb? At school the next day I haltingly mumbled the words.

"That is a very good one," said the teacher.

It was a turning point for me, and that moment is crystal clear in my mind. My father knew about a dictionary and he was right, after all. I still remember my pride and sense of exultation.

Still, the small triumphs were rare and they were not enough to balance the other miseries—until I was in the third grade. One day Miss Detrow said to us, "Class, do you know that Patty Gilboy can speak two languages? One she speaks with her voice and one with her hands. Patty, will you come up here and show the class how you can talk with your hands?"

Remembering my other humiliations, I could have died. I was sure that getting all that attention would make the teasing worse than ever. Oh, the children would be polite enough in the classroom—they wouldn't dare be mean in front of the teacher—but out on the playground it would start all over again. I dragged my feet as I left my place.

When I got up front she said, "Why don't you do the manual alphabet?"

So I signed A, B, C, D, E, F, G, and I could actually sign faster than I could talk.

She said, "Why don't you do some other signs and symbols?"

My fingers shaped the words. "Reading, writing, 1, 2, 3, 4, 5, 6, 7, 8, 9, 10," and more.

On the playground and on the way home the same children who'd made fun of me for two and a half years came up to me and said, "Hey, how do you say *Bill* in sign language? How do you say *Harry*? How do you say *Sally*? Could you teach me to talk to your mother and father?"

In the space of a few minutes Miss Detrow had turned my life around. The stuttering didn't end but for the first time I felt accepted by the other children, and I lost my fear of school. In time it even became fun.

I grew up in a hurry when I had to help my parents with ordinary business activities. If someone wanted to know when a bill would be paid, Mother would sign back that she'd pay $10 on it next month, and I'd transmit the message. Sometimes I'd have to go to a neighbor's house and ask to borrow the phone. They'd smile and say, "No, but you may use it."

I often had to run errands and sometimes I felt overwhelmed because I didn't understand all that was going on. Once when I was seven or eight Mother sent me to the store to buy a dozen ears of corn. Somehow I misunderstood and bought three or four dozen. The store clerk jammed them all into one big bag and it was very heavy, and on the way home the bag broke and the corn went sprawling all over the sidewalk. I cried while I collected it and then I hid the ears in a nearby hedge, hoping no one would find and take them. I continued to cry all the way home, where I told Mother what had happened.

She said, "I only asked for a dozen." She was gentle with me and added, "It's all right, you just didn't understand." She got two big bags and went with me to gather up the corn. We didn't take it back; I suppose we ate it for a week. I said, "Don't ever do that again, don't ever ask me to shop for you." Of course I got over it and didn't hold her to the no-shopping request.

When I was three my mother had twins, a boy and a girl—Leo Vincent and Leona Mary, who was always called Lee. Dad moved to another bed for a few months and Mom slept with a baby on each side, with a string running from each of her wrists to theirs. That way the slightest movement would awaken her and she could tend to their needs.

When she went to the basement to do the laundry she either took them with her, or if they were sleeping she timed herself and came upstairs every five minutes to check on them.

When I was six she had another girl, Dorothea Rita, or Dot. She had beautiful, naturally curly brown hair that fell into ringlets all over her head. As the baby of the family she was Dad's favorite, and all the more so because of her total beauty. He seldom disciplined her when she misbehaved as he did with the rest of us. When she wanted a quarter he would give it to her if he had it.

Fortunately all of us had normal hearing, as our parents' deafness came from childhood diseases and was not inherited. Since I was the oldest and the first to experience the world of speech, I had a lot of responsibilities with the little ones.

Our family may have been different, but we thoroughly enjoyed holidays and fun times.

Christmas was a big event for us. Mom would bake hundreds of cookies in batches of several dozen at a time, as well as great quantities of a snack mix made of Cheerios, pretzels and garlic powder. She had to ration out the cookies, three in the afternoon and three more after supper. We probably could have eaten dozens in one evening if we'd put our minds to it.

Dad always waited till the last minute to go out for the tree so we'd get a good price. The tree he brought home was invariably ugly and I would cry about it, even though Mom insisted that by the time it was decorated it would be beautiful. This was hard to believe because it was usually crooked beyond repair; it seemed that we always had the worst tree in the neighborhood. Dad would turn it around, but it looked just as terrible from the other side.

Yet it really was beautiful when decorated. Mom had the patience of Job and she took the icicles, painstakingly separated them and draped them individually over the branches. When she took the tree down she was just as patient as she removed each separate icicle and wrapped it around cardboard for the next year.

Mom and Dad would tell us to go to bed or Santa Claus wouldn't bring us any gifts. Sometimes we would leave a plate of cookies on the fireplace. We didn't have a real wood-burning fireplace, just one with a little gas stove, but that didn't present any problems for us. We didn't think of Santa coming down the chimney because we never used it. If anything, we assumed that he came in the kitchen door.

We couldn't wait to get up on Christmas morning, when we would run in and wake up Mom and Dad so we could open our presents. There were always special gifts for each of us—not a lot of gifts because we weren't wealthy, but always something we wanted and needed. Mom was a great seamstress and she made nice clothes for all of us. There was always a surprise which she must have made while we were in school. In addition to the practical gifts there were some fun things such as toys and games, and one year a bike to be shared. We went to church on Christmas morning and in the afternoon we had a festive dinner of turkey and all the trimmings.

Our Easter traditions were much simpler. Mother had saved a half dozen special cups she used only for dying the eggs on the day before Easter. Dad would hide the eggs in the back yard and we'd have to find them. We each had beautiful baskets with candy and eggs.

Mother made us girls all new outfits and they were all alike. We went to church looking quite nice, and Dad was so proud of us. We always had a big dinner on Easter, but that wasn't so different as every Sunday dinner was special.

No matter how old we got, even after we left home, those of us who lived nearby would get together with Mom and Dad for Christmas and Easter. There was never any question that we'd be there.

We also enjoyed the lesser holidays such as Halloween, which was great fun. We'd get dressed up in our costumes and then go off trick-or-treating. When we got back with our loot, Mom would take the candy away from us so we wouldn't gobble it up all at once, and then she'd dole it out to us for our lunches. She never knew that all of us would put some of it aside and hide it in our bedrooms precisely so we *could* gobble it up. Of course Mom always had candy in the house to give the other beggars, and we were pleased when there was some left.

Our few family vacations were spent visiting Mother's family in Weirton, West Virginia, or her sister Sophie in Burgettstown, Pennsylvania. We didn't do much traveling other than visiting family because it was so expensive, and because of communication problems. We loved going out of state to visit our relatives and showing off our Ohio license plates.

Aunt Sophie lived out in the country, but not on a real farm. She lived in a big old building right on the main highway. At one time it was a gas station and dance hall. Now half of the building was Aunt Sophie's house and the other half the dance hall. It must not have been used because we would go into it, run around and "have a ball."

There were lots of trucks and other traffic on the main highway so we had to be careful as we walked from her house to the little country general store. We'd go there to buy candy and ice cream and then walk back up. There was a big back yard, all wooded and with shrubs, and we loved to run around there. She also had a garden so we could count on picking fresh corn in the summer, as well as blackberries from the wealth of bushes nearby. We were also introduced to a primitive lifestyle: Aunt Sophie did not have "indoor plumbing" but a two-hole outhouse, and we had to use chamber pots at night.

Across the street from the house there was a little

hill which claimed our attention. There was a tragedy involved there. When Aunt Sophie's son was about eleven or twelve years old he was sled riding one day. He sped down that hill right into the path of a truck and was killed instantly. We were awed by the knowledge of that tragedy, but moods move quickly with children, and on the whole we had a lot of fun on that hill.

The deaf picnic was our big event and we went regularly until I was about nineteen or twenty. It was held at Mill Creek Park in Youngstown so it was very convenient for us, just a few miles from our suburban home in Boardman. People came from Pennsylvania and West Virginia and from all over Ohio. There was an amusement park right next to it, Idora Park. We could hardly wait to get there, but, of course, the parents all wanted to sit and talk after the picnic dinner. Finally about 5:00 or 6:00 p.m. the young people would say, "Come on! We want to go on the rides." They'd finally take us there.

Most of the children at the deaf picnic could hear. Their parents had become deaf after birth so it wasn't a genetic factor. Even a few who were born deaf would have hearing children. One couple had four children, and two of them could hear but their children were born deaf. Of the two who were born deaf, their children could hear, so even when it was genetic it might skip a generation.

In addition to this once-a-year regional event there were a number of activities sponsored by local clubs for the deaf. The Youngstown Silent Club was central for my parents. They went there regularly for meetings and socials, and that's where they met the other deaf couples, some of whom came to play cards with them in our home.

There were other clubs in Akron and Canton, and sometimes the Youngstown group would get together with them. There was a state club that they visited a couple of times, but they never went to the national meetings.

Mom and Dad didn't have today's wonderful technology which has been developed to help the deaf, but they learned to cope in many small ways. When we children were young they devised a method to make sure none of us ever locked ourselves in the bathroom: Mom simply hung a towel over the top of the door. It allowed us to close the door so we'd have privacy, but it couldn't shut tight enough to lock the door. Since they'd never have heard us banging to get out, this simply solved the problem before it could happen.

We had a little light in the hallway which blinked when the doorbell rang, and that was in operation until we got a dog. After that the dog would bark and run back and forth between them and the door to let them know someone was there. Now there are trained hearing ear dogs available.

The biggest help was to have hearing children who could interpret. I learned signing partly from Mother and Dad and partly from a teenage friend of ours, Fran Hetzler, whose parents were also deaf. Then I taught my brothers and sisters. Once we had the basics, others could help expand our vocabulary.

I have heard of a couple of situations where the authorities tried to take away the children of deaf parents because they didn't believe that the deaf could raise children to live in a normal world. Thank God there was never any such attempt with us. On the contrary, people in the community respected Mother and Dad and admired them for being such good parents. I was happy to learn that in both situations mentioned, the courts lost and the children were permitted to remain with their parents.

Because of recent films and television presentations, for the first time the deaf are seen as having rights. The Gallaudet University protest in the spring of 1988 also helped, when students at this university for the deaf demanded and got a deaf administrator.

My parents were not mute, but since they had lost their hearing so young they could not speak normally. You have to be able to hear the spoken word in order to imitate it. If they wanted to call us to come indoors they could do it, but it sounded strange to those who weren't used to it. Mother could speak our names more clearly, but Dad had a kind of moaning sound.

Our neighbors loved and respected them, but children were sometimes cruel. I always thought I was the only one to face the teasing and mockery because of Mother and Dad. It was only when we were all adults that I learned Leo and Lee were also subject to a good deal of taunting. None of us ever spoke about it at home, and we were not aware of what the others had faced. Only Dot was spared. She did not recall any teasing, but she did have plenty of anger toward adults who acted as though our parents were stupid. If she took Mother to the store, clerks often acted as though Mother were an idiot, simply because she couldn't hear or speak normally. Of course the rest of us also had that same anger.

When they were ten or eleven Leo and Lee really began to appreciate our parents. Before that they were sometimes embarrassed. It was that same embarrassment which kept all of us from inviting

Mother and Dad to come to school as other parents did. We were self-conscious about having them come into the classroom and sign to us, so we just never invited them. I'm sure if we'd asked they would have come.

We had typical sibling relations in our family, including fighting. We argued about whose turn it was to do the dishes or the other chores.

One time Dot yelled "Shut up!" Mother said, "I read your lips and I know what you said, and you're not allowed to say that."

I got along pretty well with the younger ones but sometimes they thought I was too bossy. Most of the fighting was just arguing, though I remember one time when we were chasing each other around the dining room table and someone had a table knife.

Like most families, we might fight among ourselves but we defended each other against outsiders. If I saw the twins being pushed around by anyone I'd go right out there and make the bullies stop, and, of course, all three of us were defensive about our little sister. If anyone even looked at her we'd beat them up. We knew Mom and Dad couldn't help so we looked after each other. Ours was basically a good neighborhood, though, and there was little real threat to any of us.

We had one bike for the four of us. Dad had bought a girl's bike, and Leo asked him why. Dad explained that there were three girls and only one boy. Sometimes Leo would take the bike early and bring it back late, and the girls were upset with him. More often he would borrow his buddy's bike.

Sometimes Dad would take Leo fishing, and, of course, he loved that. When Dad told any of us to do something he expected instant obedience. One time Leo and his friends were playing ball and Dad told him to come in. When he didn't do so, Dad went out, picked up the bat and it went flying. It broke up the game and Leo came in.

World War II had started just before I went into high school, and it brought a change. Because so many men had been drafted there was a shortage of workers, and Mother went to work as a welder at the MacKenzie Muffler Corporation. They needed women since the men were gone, and they were glad to get her. The deaf were good workers, and as they couldn't hear anyway, they didn't have to worry about noise pollution.

Dad took her to work for a few days until she found a woman who lived nearby. They became friends, and Mom asked her boss if they could be on the same shift. From that time on she'd go over to the woman's house—usually walking, or in bad weather Dad would drive her there—and then they'd ride together to work.

It must have taken a great deal of courage for her to go out into the working world after all those years at home, and to be the only deaf person in the plant. I know she must have been scared, but she had great courage and wouldn't let her fears stop her.

We quickly got used to Mom's "New Look" while she was on the job—slacks and a top and her hair wrapped up in a bandanna. Company regulations wouldn't allow her to wear her hair loose for fear she'd get it caught in the machinery.

When Mom worked I was so proud of her. I knew we needed the money, but it put a lot of responsibility on me and I didn't have her experience or organization skills. It was tough, though I never felt exploited; there was only the feeling that there was a job that had to be done.

While she was working we all had our chores. I had the job of starting supper, the girls helped with the cleaning and Leo did the outdoor work, whatever Dad needed. Dot had naturally curly hair and Mom would always put it in ringlets. When she went to work I had the job of combing Dot's hair, and I wasn't very good at it. Mom did it so beautifully, and Dot hated having me work on it because I did such a bad job.

Teenager

High school was a good time for me. I was outgoing, but didn't date as I wasn't really that good looking and no one wanted to take me out. There was just one arranged date in my four years, and it was a disaster. A new boy had come to school and we had become friendly. He didn't have time to get settled in or to know people when someone fixed him up with me. He didn't really want to go with me but he was new and didn't feel like he should say no. You could see that he was forced into this, and it's simply awful to be out with a date and know that he wants to be somewhere else. Between the time he accepted and the time of the dance he fell in love with a gorgeous blond girl in our class. During the whole time at the dance he was looking across the room at her. It was a terrible, terrible evening for me.

I had lots of girl friends and I'd ham it up and act crazy. There were sixteen of us in a Pep Club, which we formed for our own level because we weren't in the top social and economic group. I also had friends among the boys, but they looked on me as a buddy and the feeling was mutual. I enjoyed them as friends but I wasn't ready for more than that.

When it came time for the senior play, Mr. George Bohn, the director, said to me, "We have a part in the play for a maid. She just has a few lines, and she gets some laughs. Would you like to be in it?"

I said, "I don't know if I could say the words without stuttering."

Then he handed me the part and said, "Why don't you look it over, and if there's anything you might stumble on we can change the lines so you're more comfortable with the part." There were no more than a half dozen lines.

There were certain sounds that I blocked on, especially words that started with vowels, anything starting with an "a"—attitude, action, and the like. We changed a few words and I played the part successfully and got lots of laughs. What a wonderful man he was to take the time to work with me.

I was a skinny, graceless, homely child, with one shoulder higher than the other. Mother always fixed my clothes so it wasn't so noticeable.

In my freshman year of high school they had a new type of X-Ray to check us for tuberculosis. That year the chest X-Rays went clear through to the spine. They found cases of scoliosis, or curvature of the spine, all over the country. Several of these cases were in the Youngstown area and I was one of them. The school sent a note home to my parents to take me to the doctor. They were so afraid that I might have TB.

Our family physician had word from the school, and he sent me to an orthopedist. He said that I had an almost perfect "S" curve and it was an old condition, dating from birth or a childhood injury. Surgery would be necessary, but he said if I were careful it might be postponed until after graduation. Today that condition can be handled with a brace, but then it required an operation. I went to the hospital for surgery just a month after I was graduated from high school. They put me in a body cast to straighten my spine. Then during surgery they removed some bone from my leg and it was fused to my spine, so I was immobilized and could use only one arm and leg for the next ten and a half months. All that time I was in the cast, flat on my back during the day, and I had to be turned over at night to implement healing.

When the ambulance brought me home I had to be hauled through a window. I was downstairs so Mother could care for me, but I had nightmares that someone could come through the window and get me while I was helpless. I could visualize the window being opened and a man coming in. I had a light switch and could pull it, and hoped Dad would see the light. When I pulled it on, of course, there was no one there, but it wakened my parents and they came to check on me. Then I felt badly about disturbing their sleep. I still have vivid memories of feeling so helpless and thinking that if some man comes in and does something to me, Mom and Dad won't hear me. I was completely immobilized in that cast. I couldn't get up or stand; all I could do was lie in bed, and I counted the days till I could get out of it.

I went crazy with the itching inside the cast. I realize this is quite normal, and anyone who has ever experienced a broken bone surrounded by a cast can tell the same story: the itching is just terrible. I would find anything I could use and shove it down inside the cast. When I think now of some of the dangerous things I used, I'm horrified at what I did, for I could have injured my body or the stitches. I remember once taking my dinner knife and scratching and thinking how good it felt. My favorite was a ruler. One day Mother came in and saw me digging inside the cast with it, and as she took it away from me she said, "Absolutely not!"

At different times my friends and my brother and sisters did what they could to help. They used to scratch at the top of the cast and dig at it with their fingernails, and the noise of it would affect my imagination. They would try to take my mind off the itching. I remember at night when I was alone and it would start. I would sing, I would try to think of other things—did you ever try to avoid thinking of an itch?—and finally I would find something on the night stand, send it in and start scratching. Even now I think how lucky I am to be able to scratch any part of my body that I wish!

College

After my year of healing I went to Youngstown College. All through school I had been plagued by my stuttering, and I decided that this was the time to do something about it. Now I said to myself, "You are entering college and nobody knows who you are or that you stutter. You are going to be adept at avoiding the words and sounds that make you stutter." Once I set my goal in words it began to come true. When I slipped occasionally I joked about it and no one really knew. Eventually I mastered it through a combination of increased self esteem and raw determination. My self esteem rose as I became popular. I knew I was somebody special and it was okay that my parents were deaf. My friends loved and admired Mother and Dad, and many of them learned sign language from me so they could communicate with them. When I was invited to join a sorority I knew I was accepted and that I belonged, and that did wonders for me. Today I no longer block on any sounds. Every once in a while when I'm talking to a group I have the feeling I should tell this. I explain that I believe in miracles, tell my story, then say that they too can have miracles. Often people hearing it have come to me afterward and said that it helped immensely.

I loved college. It was so different from high school, where they like you for what you have. In college they like you for what you are. One of the exciting things was making new friends and joining a good local sorority, which was later affiliated with the national Alpha Omicron Pi. That was great for my social life but not so good for my grades. My academic record was poor for the first two years because I was a bit of a good timer. I had made one of the highest English grades in the entrance exam in Youngstown College history, yet I had a warning from the Education Department because my grades had dropped so low.

My counselor said, "The entrance exam results and the grades you are getting now show me one thing: you are fooling around and not studying. Either you are going to settle down or you are not going to be a teacher." When I walked out of there I was devastated. I thought to myself, "All my life, all I've ever wanted to do was to teach." I had admired so many of my former teachers and wanted to be just like them. I asked myself, "What are you going to do, Pat—throw your whole life away for a few parties and fun when you're going to college?" I decided against that.

I couldn't even face my parents. I was so ashamed because I knew they had sacrificed to send me to college. How could I let them down like this?

I realized that all it meant was settling down for two years and then I'd have the rest of my future assured. I was not aware that one could set goals and learn to study. Today it is possible to take courses or workshops in study skills, as well as having books and tapes available, but in my day I had to learn it on my own.

Believe me, from that day on I studied more, worked more, and partied less. I began to get good grades and was accepted into the Education Department, and I made the honor roll the last two years.

II.

I Become a Teacher

After graduation I applied to the Youngstown schools, an excellent system with higher pay than many of the surrounding systems. There was a lot of competition, with applications from people from some of the best colleges and universities.

When I went for the interview the Superintendent of Schools asked me why I wanted to be a teacher. I told him about my parents being deaf, about being the first-born child, and being responsible for my brother and sisters all of my life. Teaching just seemed so natural to me because in a way I had been a teacher for my parents. On top of that, I really loved children.

He hired me on the spot. I think he felt that because of my unique experiences I would have something to offer children with limited backgrounds.

I was a second grade teacher and loved it. My goal was to make it the best year possible for each child in the class. This appeared to be successful, and I seemed to be "made" for teaching. It was easy to work with the children—I was full of enthusiasm and ideas, and there was plenty of opportunity to try them out.

One of the most important ideas was to enlist the cooperation of all the children to help make everyone feel wanted and loved and accepted.

There was a boy who had epileptic seizures. There was never any warning—he just went into them. The nurse told me to keep a tongue depressor handy, and to lay him on the floor when he had a seizure. At that time they would stick the tongue depressor into the child's mouth to keep him from swallowing his tongue, a procedure not generally in use today.

I told the children, "We're not going to cry when Billy does this. We're going to be calm and not make him feel like he's different." When he suddenly went "Aaaaahhh . . ." I'd rush back there with the tongue depressor and lay him down. I'd tell the children, "Look the other way. Billy's going to be all right." He'd lay there and shake for a few minutes. The nurse was in the building only three days a week, and if she was there I'd send one of the children after her.

Another time the principal told me, "You're going to get Eddie Jones. Mrs. Wilson had him and he has kicked her in the legs so many times she can barely walk. I can't give him to Miss Miller because she would have a heart attack and die." Mrs. Wilson was elderly and frail, and Miss Miller was very heavy.

Eddie was in the office every single day from his first day in the first grade. He was equally bad at home and school. He set fire to his garage. He had a vicious father who beat him unmercifully. His mother forced him out of the house with a broom every morning, swatting him all the way up the street to school.

His favorite trick was to sharpen the pencil till the point was as sharp as a needle, then go up to a girl and just shove it in her arm. The nurse was digging lead out of arms all week.

The principal said, "I don't know what to do with him, so you're just going to have to take him. He is awful. I have paddled him but he has bitten and kicked me. He has no respect for authority."

I asked when he would come to my class.

"Tomorrow," she said.

That afternoon before the class went home I said, "Children, we're getting Eddie Jones tomorrow."

They said, "Oh no, he's going to ruin our room." Everyone had something to say about him. "I live on his street. He is so bad, wait till I tell you what he did to my brother." The stories went on and on.

"Wait a minute," I said. "We're going to help him. We're going to do something for Eddie that no one has done before. When he sharpens his pencil and shoves it into your arm, Mary, you're not going to scream, you're just going to come up quietly and say to me, 'Look what Eddie did,' and I'm going to take care of it."

We had tables then, with three children on each side. There his favorite thing was to take a thick black crayon and run it on the others' papers and ruin them.

"When he wrecks your paper don't cry out," I said. "Just quietly turn the paper over and raise your hand and I'll give you another. In other words we are not going to give him attention negatively, we're going to give it to him positively. I'm going to touch him a lot and tell him how nice he looks, and give him jobs to do."

"It's *my* job to wash the blackboard," protested one little girl.

"I know, but let Eddie do it once in a while," I said.

"He'll just throw the bucket," she continued.

I said, "Well, we're going to give him a chance, aren't we?"

The first couple of days he did all those things and the children were like perfectly tuned little actors and actresses. They were just wonderful and they'd whisper to me when things went wrong.

They said, "We're so happy to have you, Eddie." He said, "YEAH?" They said, "We certainly are."

It was a riot. After two weeks the principal came down and said to me, "What are you doing in here? Eddie has not been to the office in two weeks." I said, "We're loving him, we're doing positive things with him."

She said, "Whatever it is, keep it up because it's working."

At the next parents' night in came a big blond woman. "Miss Gilboy?" "Yes," I said. "I'm Eddie Jones' mother." "Yes," I replied, "How are you?" "I don't know what you're doing," she said, "but I don't even have to beat him with the broom every morning to get him to go to school. He just walks out the door on his own."

That was my biggest success. Eddie continued to progress during the year, but I lost track of him after that and I don't know what ever happened to him. At least for one year of his life he was treated with dignity.

Another idea I carried out was to visit every child's home. One of my professors had said, "You cannot teach a child effectively until you know what kind of home he has." I decided to try it, but the other teachers didn't think much of that and one said, "You know, some of these parents may not want you in their homes. Some of the children live in shacks. Do you think you have a right to go in there?"

"When I go I'm not going to look at their shacks," I said. "I'm just going to visit with their parents." Each year I visited every child's home. I loved it and learned a lot, and I had some nice experiences. There was one boy whom I was always correcting—"John, sit up straight. John, pay attention." When I was in his home I discovered that his parents did that all the time and here I was doing the same thing. I changed completely with him and never nagged him again. When I stopped nagging, he turned around.

Of course I was always interested in any children who had speech defects, and I hoped I could prevent them from going through the miseries I'd had when growing up. At one time I had eleven children with speech defects in my room. We had a wonderful speech therapist for the school system and we hit it off well. When I decided to try to help these youngsters she gave me some practical suggestions. I was working with them with mirrors, helping them see what happened when they lisped or stuttered. Unfortunately the families weren't cooperative, and they said all the wrong things: "Slow down." "Think what you're going to say." These are the worst things you can say to stutterers because it makes them self-conscious and they stumble more than ever.

Meanwhile Elizabeth Miller, another speech therapist, was also working with the system. When I was a ninth grader I was sent to her and she was convinced my problem was psychological, a guilty response for being ashamed of my parents. I didn't continue with her and I don't think she ever realized I was that freshman who came into her office. Now she used me as an example of clearing up speech defects because I cared enough to spend time with the children.

One thing my second graders liked was that I always wore nice looking clothes and accessories. When I was a child, Mother had always made my clothes, and while they were nice they weren't stylish. When I started earning my own money I went a bit wild on clothes and built up quite a wardrobe. Long earrings were in then, and the children always watched to see what I was wearing.

I felt so happy and fulfilled in my work, but it wasn't just the work. I was also hopelessly in love.

III.

New Directions

Not long after starting at Youngstown College, Tony Vivo and I met, but it definitely was not "love at first sight." As a matter of fact, I was using him to try to develop another romance. I was in love with a football player who was also named Tony, and though he seemed to like me I didn't run into him often enough to suit me. Every day at 3:00 the players came to a dressing room and got into football gear, then went by bus to a nearby high school to practice. At that time the college did not have a stadium or practice field.

Next to the dressing room was an office with "Anthony Vivo, Ticket Director" on the door. With my wily mind I thought if I could meet this Mr. Vivo then I could get here a little before 3:00 every day and see my football player. I asked someone if he knew Anthony Vivo. He said, "Sure, everybody knows Tony Vivo."

"I want to meet him," I said.

"He's here every day at noon," was the answer. So the next day I got there at noon and he introduced us. My immediate impression was what a very nice man he was. There was no love interest whatever.

That afternoon at a quarter of three I ran over to his office and said, "Hi, Mr. Vivo. I met you today and I just wanted to see your office." It was nothing but an overgrown closet with a desk and a secretary there. We talked for a few minutes, just light banter on my part. Then the football players came in and my football player said, "Hi there, what are you doing here?"

I said, "Mr. Vivo is a good friend of mine."

"That's nice," he said. "Do you want to go out tomorrow night?"

So I accomplished my objective. I would go over there every other day about the same time. Some three months later, Tony Vivo asked me to go to the bonfire rally on Friday night. That was a fun thing before the big game. Because he was older I didn't think he was asking me out for a date, so I told all my friends that we had a ride to the rally. When he came to pick me up, five of my friends climbed in the car with me. I didn't even look at him so I didn't notice if he was surprised. Of course, he also had to take us all home and we were scattered all over—one lived in Niles and one in Girard, both Youngstown suburbs. I'm sure he didn't get home much before 3:00 a.m.

Monday morning he said to me, "I don't want to take your friends out, I just want to take you out."

I said, "Oh, all right."

The next thing I knew one of my friends came up and said, "My mother knows him. Do you know how old he is?"

I knew he was older, but figured him to be about 25, and since I was 19 I didn't think that was too bad.

She said, "Pat, he's 34 years old."

I groaned. "Gosh, I don't think my mother's going to let me go out with him."

She said, "Now I've got something else to tell you—he's divorced."

I said, "Oh, no."

She added, "He's got a little girl."

"Now I *know* my mother won't let me go," I said.

I went home and told her, "Tony Vivo is asking me out and I don't know what to do." Then I told her what I knew about him. He was a Catholic, but because of his age and divorced state she was concerned.

She said, "Be very careful. Tread slowly and get to know this man well. Don't make any rash decisions."

He came to the house and met my parents, and they liked him immediately. I liked him too, more and more, and soon it went from like to love.

Tony was a graduate in social work and held a full time job in that field, but he also worked full time at the college as the ticket director in charge of tickets for all sports. He was 5'9", well built, and nice looking.

We dated for seven years, during my four years of college and three of teaching. During most of that time he also dated Mary, Betty, Sally, Carrie, and others. He had lots of girl friends, but he was quite honest with me. Every time I even mentioned marriage he said, "I don't want any part of that." It took four years for him to love me back. I probably just grew on him, for some time between my last year of college and the first year of teaching he fell in love.

The Youngstown schools required teachers to have a physical exam every year to make sure they were in shape to work with the children. The third year they discovered a lump on my breast. I asked to hold off hospitalization until December when we'd have a two week break, so they scheduled me for surgery on December 16th. I learned about it in September and told Tony then.

Tony and I went out on December 6th. That evening he said that whatever happened he wanted to marry me, and he gave me a ring.

The "whatever" turned out to be benign and we were married the following spring on a beautiful day in May which was also my parents' anniversary. Our marriage took place in a Protestant church, however. My priest, who didn't actually know that much about canon law, said that if I married him I would be excommunicated because he was divorced. He didn't bother to check the circumstances, which would have permitted an annulment and a marriage within the Catholic Church.

Those circumstances have since changed, but at that time the ruling was that if there was a marriage between a Catholic and a Protestant in a Protestant Church, the Catholic Church did not recognize the marriage. That was the case with Tony's first marriage.

Since we were both well known we had a big wedding. All my little second graders came to it, along with some 250 other people.

As Protestants from Catholic families we felt like fish out of water. Two years later when we learned that the annulment and remarriage were possible we were quite happy about it, and we made arrangements with a wonderful priest who had a firm knowledge of canon law. He arranged for us to go to confession and then to have a quiet remarriage in Sacred Heart Church on the east side of Youngstown.

His brother and sister-in-law, Steve and Helen Vivo, were our witnesses. It was a joyful time because it seemed as though we were back together with both our families. We had a small dinner afterward with Helen and Steve, but I don't remember my parents being there. Perhaps they were baby-sitting.

The Camp

Tony was boys' director at Christ Mission Settlement and camp director at Christ Mission Camp. The camp job was an extension of the settlement work. He had been attending the camp since he was five or six years old, when he was brought in because he was from a poor family. He had worked his way up to counselor, then finally to director. He spent every summer there from 1949 until it closed in 1958.

It was a beautiful camp in Canfield, located on Leffingwell Road and set back from the road. Gorgeous homes lined the road. There were two other camps out there at this time, including one for the Boy Scouts. I think the camp had some fifty or sixty acres which had a farm on one part. In another section a farmer lived on a self-sustaining farm, in another there was a large garden, and finally there was the camp itself.

It was in a wooded area and had a swimming pool and two large dormitories, built in a "W" effect. One wing was for the boys and one for the girls. In between there was a huge dining room and behind that, the kitchen. In front there was a lobby with a piano, where most of our meetings were held. There was also a little workshop for crafts. Craft sessions were held all over, however—in various rooms, a corner of the cafeteria, a corner of the dorm, or perhaps outside around the camp grounds.

There was a large open field by the swimming pool, and on the other side of the field was a big auditorium with a stage on it. That is where we held the big meetings and church services, had visiting groups, and put on plays.

A flagpole stood in the middle of the field. I'll never forget it! Every year the rope rotted from the weather and every year my husband would shinny up that huge flagpole and replace the rope, then shinny back down, all to the delight of the children. They loved to watch him do that. It was quite scary. I can't believe now that he did it, but he was agile and in good condition.

As Tony's wife I was now very much a part of the camp and a member of the staff. We moved out there around the middle of May to get it ready to open about June 10th. We had to mow all the grass and clean the buildings. He did most of that himself, with just a few staff.

We lived in a huge bedroom right off the kitchen; I remember it vividly. There wasn't much to it—a great big bed, an old dresser and a big sink—but it was enough for our needs. We didn't spend much time there. Camp ended in late August and we stayed into September to close up. We boarded the windows, drained the pool, and did the rest of the necessary closing chores, and sometimes it was late when we moved back into our apartment.

One hundred and fifty children were selected to go there and stay for nine weeks. When they arrived their clothes were replaced with camp outfits, and they had good food and fun for the entire summer.

Some came from poor families, while others had been neglected or abused and taken over by the Juvenile Court. The Children's Services Bureau placed them in the camp for the summer while the court decided what to do with them. They no longer do this today, but it was easier then. At that time, if Juvenile Court workers saw a child running the streets they'd go right to the parents and say, "That child belongs at Christ Mission Camp. We'll see if we can get him in there."

I remember one particular family where the parents had an argument and the father shot the mother. There was no place for the children to go, so the Children's Services sent them all to Christ Mission for nine weeks.

The children lived on crowded city streets, in ghettos and troubled homes, and this was paradise for them. They had never had such clean fresh air. Back then Youngstown was a mill town so these children sometimes lived right near the steel mills and were used to nothing but black smoke. We were about fourteen miles from the city and had wonderful air out there.

The children were on a regular schedule, most of them for the first time in their lives. Some of them had run the streets and just grabbed a sandwich wherever they could; they'd never sat down to a planned dinner before. Seeing salt and pepper and butter on the table was a new experience for them.

Because we had both worked with children and loved them, Tony and I wanted a big family. Sometimes people think this was because of our Catholic upbringing, but that had nothing to do with it. We just felt that the ideal home was one full of children. Since Tony was older we wanted to start a family right away. I had a miscarriage early on, but when the children started coming they came steadily— seven of them in eight and a half years.

Before we were married he had been living in a two-bedroom upstairs apartment, and that was our first home. The stairs were steep and I was soon pregnant with Anthony, so we wanted to get on the first floor as soon as possible. Anthony was a toddler and I was pregnant with Allison when the downstairs apartment became available. The new apartment was larger and it was cheerful and pleasant, just right for our beginning family. When Allison arrived we put her in a playpen in the dining room and we also used it as her bed, while Anthony had the other bedroom. By keeping the two separate they didn't wake each other with crying.

When Alicia was on the way we realized that this charming apartment would not stretch enough, so we started house-hunting. We found just what we needed in Boardman, the Youngstown suburb where I grew up, and we are still there today. The first floor had a large living room, a nice family room, a dining room, kitchen, three bedrooms and a bath. Upstairs there was an apartment the previous owner had built for her elderly mother. It had a living room, dining room, kitchen, bedroom and bath. Our friends and families wondered what we would do with such a big house and why we would need all that space.

When Tony and I first saw the attractive little upstairs apartment we thought of it as a possibility for my parents when they could no longer maintain their own home. Tony, Mother and Dad had a great deal of love and respect for each other. He never mastered sign language but he managed to communicate with them, and he was especially close to Mother. He was

quite comfortable with the thought of having them
live with us. As it turned out, that idea never had a
chance to get off the ground because we started filling up the rooms with babies.

Alicia was the next to arrive, then Allan, Angela,
Andrew and Andrea, as close as stairsteps. And of
course Janis, Tony's first daughter, spent some time
with us. She was very much a part of the family and
I loved her just as much as the children I bore.

Sometimes people ask us why our children's
names all begin with A. We didn't plan it that way—
it just happened. As the first boy, Anthony was
named for his father, but we didn't want a "Junior"
and Tony had no middle name. Anthony's middle
name was Patrick after my Uncle Patrick, and it is the
masculine form of my name, Patricia.

I'd always loved the name Allison and wanted to
use it if I ever had a daughter. Her middle name is
Lee, after my sister. Alicia Mary got her name because Alicia was another favorite name, and Mary is
after my mother. Then we realized we had three A's
without ever intending it, so we thought we would
just continue the tradition. The middle names would
honor family members. Allan Stephen was after
Tony's father and Angela Stella was after his mother.

I had been saving Andrew and Andrea in case we
ever had twins, a real possibility because we had
them on both sides of our families. By the time we
came to our sixth child it seemed highly unlikely that
there would be any twins, so that boy was named
Andrew Leo after my father and brother. Andrea Rita
was given my sister Dot's middle name.

Whenever I called them by their full names they
knew I was angry and they had better shape up, as
normally the middle name was never used. They had

nicknames for each other Lison, Gela, Drea, Al, Antonio, Drew, Lish. Neither Tony nor I used these names, and if anyone called and asked for someone by a nickname I'd reply that they had the wrong number, as no Al lives here.

It seemed as though I was always pregnant. People would see me on the street and ask, "Is this the same one or is it another one?" Once at a party a man commented, "George Washington was the Father of our country, and now I know who the Mother is." These things never bothered me because I loved being pregnant. Marriage and motherhood were tremendously fulfilling for me. I didn't have to do everything alone. Tony was a wonderful father and was always there when I needed him, and he saw that I had every kind of labor-saving device to make my housework easier and lighter. He also did all the grocery shopping and bought all the children's clothes until they got older and more clothes-conscious, and asked him to stop buying them. He'd had years of experience doing these things when he ran the camp.

As the children arrived the house had to be stretched for them. Tony has always been very handy with tools, so he tore down the apartment and turned most of it into a dormitory bedroom. It had four twin beds with four little bedside tables, four white dressers, and four lamps. Word of this got out and sometimes friends would stop and announce that they wanted to see the famous dormitory.

The three boys stayed downstairs and the four girls were in the dorm. We kept the original upstairs bedroom intact and used it as Janis's room when she stayed with us. At other times it doubled as a guest room.

Tony continued to develop his carpentry skills, which was a good thing. He wasn't making very much and remodeling was so expensive that we couldn't have done it otherwise. With his expertise and the help of some skilled friends we made other changes. The wall between the back patio and the tiny little family room came down and we made it into a 24' x 24' family room with a cut stone corner fireplace. This was our favorite room and the children spent most of their time there. It had the television, a big study table with five chairs where they did their homework, and the fireplace, where they could sit around and stay warm on a cold winter night.

As the house filled with children it also filled with noise and clutter. When toys and friends were added to the child population already there, you can see that there was no surplus room. Then one day we looked at the kitchen and every place was taken at the table, the high chair over in the corner was filled, and I was pregnant. I said to Tony, "Where are we going to put this baby?" He replied, "Well, it's time to knock out the wall in the kitchen." So he did. Now we have a huge kitchen with a long table, 101" x 48", with twelve seats around it. At the same time he enlarged the garage to a triple one. He also built a huge walk-in closet for the children to hang up all their coats and keep their galoshes, with room for their lunch boxes as well.

Tony could do anything, and when things went wrong he repaired them immediately. It didn't matter if it were a malfunctioning lamp, a toaster that wouldn't work, or a broken window—he had them all back in order within twenty-four hours. He was always fixing the toaster. With our big family we had a large four-slice one, and the children would enthusiastically shove bread into it with all their might and it would jam up the works. Without Tony our repair bills would have been astronomical.

He would fix their notebooks when the rings didn't close or open correctly. He often worked on dresser drawers and they would be stacked up in the garage waiting their turn to be repaired, sanded down and put back into use. When the children were in a hurry they yanked out the drawers and periodically broke them.

And doorknobs. They would fall off and he'd put them back on again. I went into my bedroom once to get dressed and I closed the door. When I got ready to come out I couldn't get the door open again. Thank goodness my husband was home because he had to work on the other side about twenty minutes to get me out.

We learned the hard way to dismantle the locks so they wouldn't work. Once the children locked themselves into the upstairs bedroom. Tony had to get a ladder and climb in through the upstairs bathroom to get to them, and needless to say he was very angry. From then on he made sure none of the locks worked, especially in the bathroom, so if the children were angry with us or having a tantrum they couldn't hole up and make a fort of it. The one exception was the downstairs bathroom where we had a little gadget that would open it from the outside.

Bed slats were another commodity in need of frequent repair. Today most beds have box springs, but back then the bed frame had wooden slats across it and the open springs lay over them. The mattress topped it all, and a high-flying youngster might make a running jump from across the room, land in the middle, and instead of being propelled toward the ceiling, end up instead on a collapsed bed. All this was accompanied by the sound of the weakest slat being broken. Tony made frequent pilgrimages to the lumber yard to pick up wood pieces which would serve as replacement slats.

People who came to our home were always surprised at how well-maintained it was. They'd say, "You'd never know that seven children lived here."

When we remodeled or added on to the house Tony would bring in a carpenter, electrician and plumber to do the basic work. After the main shell was up he finished all the rest, including putting up the wallboard, ceilings and light fixtures, followed by painting and staining.

Tony was more than a good handyman, however— he was an outstanding father as well. He was home a lot then and he helped both with the children and the house. The children were attractive and good-looking, and he was so proud of them that he wanted to take them everywhere and show them off— sometimes even to places they shouldn't be, so I had to stop him.

For instance, I never believed my children should be taken to wedding receptions. I thought this was a place for adults, since there was drinking going on, adult conversation, and it was not at all suitable for children. When we had parties at home I believed the children should be introduced and then sent to bed, as this also wasn't the best place for them. I thought they were too young to hear or see some of the things that were going on.

Their nightly baths were a ritual which required both of us. We filled up the tub and threw in one kid, two kids, and then a third. I'd scrub them, then hand them to Tony and he'd dry them. If they were able to dress themselves he'd send them to do that; if not, they waited till I was finished with the seventh one. Then I put on their diapers and got them all ready for bed. It was mass production. As the water got dirty we simply let it out and filled it up again, whether it was the second child, fourth child or fifth child.

It was important for me to have the evening for myself, so we convinced them that seven was the time to go to bed. We tried to get started on the baths at six but sometimes we ran a little late if we'd been out on errands or attending meetings.

Someone once asked how I taught them sex education. I don't recall ever giving them formal sessions on it, but I always answered their questions as they came up, with the language and details depending on their age and understanding. Our children were used to seeing each other run around nude. As soon as any child looked at another and asked, "What's that?" I'd say, "Well, you're old enough to take your bath alone now." They were used to seeing me pregnant every year. They knew that I had a baby growing in my womb and they knew that when I went to the hospital I would deliver the baby. When they asked where, I told them clearly what part of the body the baby came from. They saw me nurse all my children and it was a normal, natural thing for them.

When one of my sons was three or four years old we were all sitting around the dinner table one evening, and in the middle of the meal my son opened up a clenched fist to reveal three nickels. He said to all of us, "I don't care how many times she wants to look at it, I'm not going to let her."

We all stopped short and looked at him. At that time we had a little girl in the neighborhood who was probably nine or ten and who lived in a house full of adults, parents and grandparents. There were no other children. Mentioning her by name he said, "She takes me in the back yard by the tree and pulls my pants down and looks at my penis, and then she gives me a nickel."

I took his hand and said, "Let's go!" and we marched to that neighbor's house and knocked on the door. I told my story and they brought the young lady forward. She denied everything, of course, and her family insisted that my son must be lying.

I said, "I'm sure my son couldn't make up a story like that." Then I looked at the girl and said, "Don't ever do that again."

We marched back home and sat back down at the dinner table. By then the other children had finished eating and left. I was too flustered to eat any more and I gathered up the dishes and went over to the sink. The more I thought of that incident, the more it bothered me. I thought, we ought to use this opportunity to teach him about the sacredness of his body, so I said to Tony, "Talk to him."

My laid-back, cool husband looked at him and said, "Next time, son, charge a dollar." I couldn't believe what I heard. "I'm not letting you near our kids until they are at least twenty-one," I told him.

When the children asked questions about sex I did not avoid them, no matter where we were or who we were with. I may have said to them, "When we get home I want to elaborate on this a little more," because I could sometimes sense that the other people were a little uncomfortable. At times we got into long conversations about human sexuality, and there were lots of questions.

When they started dating I was very direct with them. While there were no planned talks it came up very naturally in a family gathering. We have good solid talks today even though they are older. I give my views and they give theirs, and many times we disagree.

Whenever I went into the hospital to have my babies, Mother stayed home with the children. When I came from the hospital she made sure the next meal was ready and she stayed a couple of hours. The next morning she was back to help me cook and clean and take care of the children.

Sometimes when she came to visit me I would be so ashamed because the house was such a mess, just full of clutter. In the first fifteen minutes she was there I would look around and suddenly realize that things were all straightened up. In her quiet, lovely way of doing things she had picked up the clutter and gone downstairs to throw a load of laundry in the washer. Then she'd come into the kitchen, peel some potatoes and put some meat in for supper, all in the space of a few minutes. Meanwhile I was busy tending to one or two of the children.

She had a way of quietly doing these things without getting in my way, without making me feel lazy or usurping my duties. I can't explain it. She was just there making things so easy for me and lightening my load. She was that quiet solid wall of warmth and strength that I could lean on whenever I needed, and I could stand up straight when I felt that I needed to. I cannot describe in words what my mother did for me.

Even though it took a great deal of energy just to be around small children, and Mother was getting along in years, she still wanted to baby-sit for them. That allowed us to have an active social life.

While the children were in school I was active in PTA. I was also in two card clubs, so I went out twice a month to play cards. Just talking to other women about things other than diapers, bottles and babies was marvelous.

Tony was in forty-six organizations. He was very active in the Lions Club, Easter Seals, Retarded Children's Association, Cancer Society, the Democratic Party—everything. Each group had special events: an annual dance, a ladies' night or a special dinner, so, of course, we went out a lot. I loved it and it was good for me to get away from the children and enjoy myself.

Holidays were important in our family, though they were quite different from my own childhood experience. My heritage was Irish and Serbian but our family celebrations did not draw from either one. Tony's family followed their Italian background much more closely. They always had a traditional Christmas Eve dinner with different kinds of fish. We would spend Christmas Eve with them and dinner was followed by a visit from Santa.

Tony paid a bundle for an official-looking Santa Claus suit and an authentic-looking beard, which he wore on this occasion. The beard completely covered his face, and with his gloves and high boots not one part of his body showed. When the children were little I don't think they made any connection between Santa and Daddy. As they got older they were a bit more suspicious and began to look around the room for their father. From then on we would have one of his brothers wear the outfit. One of the brothers couldn't disguise himself very well, and we heard one of his children say, "I think that's Daddy!"

Sometimes we would have a friend play the part and that would really confuse the children. Finally we explained that since Santa couldn't be everywhere at once, these were his helpers. The older children had obviously figured things out long before, but they covered up nicely and pretended that it was all real.

Whether we were at his family's house or later at our own, Santa was a tradition on that day. He'd have a packaged gift for each child, and as he pulled it out we'd deliver it to the right person.

Since we had to wait till the children were in bed and asleep to make the final preparations, we would be up until three or four in the morning putting their toys together. Tony would momentarily lose his religion while he swore that they left out a screw or a part, but, of course, they didn't. When he calmed down and took it apart he'd see that he'd put it together wrong. It's one thing to be a handyman around the house, and it's something else to try to put kids' toys together.

While he was doing that I was wrapping presents, and it felt like the wrapping went on forever. Once I ran out of paper and Tony said, "You didn't!" I said, "Yes I did." So he said, "Use last year's paper." Other years when I ran out I'd use newspaper or whatever I could find that was big enough. The children didn't really care because they ripped open the gifts at lightning speed.

There was such joy in the morning. "C'mon Mommy, wake up, wake up! C'mon Daddy, wake up—come on down, we have to open up all the presents!"

Mother and Dad always came over on Christmas day. One year we lined up all the children and said, "Grandma and Grandpa, we have a Christmas present for you." Then everybody signed "Merry Christmas and a Happy New Year, Grandma and Grandpa." My parents were so moved that the children would learn to sign that message, and everyone cried for joy.

We were a normal family and there were times when the children fought, when they hated each other, they smacked and kicked each other and they chased each other. When that happened I put them in their rooms. I had hairy days when nothing went right when they knocked a hole in the wall or pushed over a beautiful lamp and broke it. There were few days that I didn't greet Tony with "You'll never believe what happened. . . ." He spent the evening fixing the things the children had broken that day.

I loved it when my children got into school. On a practical level I loved having one less child at home to care for. They had an excellent school system in Boardman and all of our children did well. There was a child in nearly every grade when they were all registered, and the teachers were fascinated with the Vivo kids and their different personalities.

There's one thing they don't warn you about when your child enters kindergarten, and that is that Show and Tell can be hazardous to a mother's reputation.

In my book, once a year for Show and Tell is a brilliant idea and once a month is a good idea. But when my son entered kindergarten his teacher had Show and Tell every single day. Every day my son was taking a big book or a big truck or a big game to Show and Tell.

His object was always so big he couldn't carry it far, so he couldn't walk to school and I had to drive him. I usually had on my old flannel nightgown with a hole in the elbow, with the half thought/half prayer that nothing would happen to the car because I couldn't get out looking like that. I used to argue with him every morning, "Do you *have* to take this big thing to Show and Tell?

One day he said, "I'm going to take this key chain."

I said, "That's a good idea." It was small so he could carry it and walk to school and save me the trip. Two and a half hours later he bounded through the field yelling at me. He said the teacher said that it wasn't very nice. I could hardly wait till he got to me and I looked at it. It was a keychain with half of a toilet seat on it, with the words, "For my half-assed friend."

"What happened?" I asked.

He said, "I stood up and said my mother said it was a good idea for me to bring this."

Then, of course, I went to my first PTA meeting and met his teacher.

"Hello, I'm Mrs. Vivo," I told her.

"I know who you are," she said.

In spite of that bad beginning, I loved PTA and became very active in it. I had all of the jobs in turn: program chair, membership chair, treasurer, vice president, president, and I did these things in all three schools where my children were involved. I'm still in PTA as a life member, and I speak to PTA groups across the country.

We were an outgoing, verbal, laughing family—and loud. The neighbors would say, "Boy, he has a daughter over there who hits high C when she cries!" But for heaven's sake, children are going to make noise.

We were in a neighborhood of older, retired people. I had fifteen free babysitters there, but never realized it at the time. I'd get calls like this: "Mrs. Vivo, do you know that your son has just picked all the geraniums in your front yard and is throwing them out on the street?" Or, "Mrs. Vivo, your daughter's on the roof." Another friend called to report a peculiar phenomenon going on in my bedroom, which faced the street. I had cafe curtains there, so the top half was just clear window. She said, "Mrs. Vivo, I think your children are doing something in your bedroom because all we see is their heads." I went upstairs and I don't know how they didn't destroy the mattress, because they were using it as a trampoline. As they popped up, all the neighbors could see were their heads.

We tried vacations, but every time we went on one our marriage almost broke up. They stopped being our children and became *my* children. We always had a station wagon but with seven children it was still cramped.

I'll never forget going down to Winston-Salem, North Carolina. One of our friends owned a motel there and said we could go down and stay free. That was the only way we could afford vacations. This was a fourteen hour drive and we had all the children packed into the wagon, all the suitcases packed on top, and there were mattresses and pillows in the back.

We pulled out of our drive and were almost to the end of the block when Andrew said, "Are we almost there? I have to vomit." That's the way the whole rest of the trip went.

"He's looking at me."

"He's touching me."
"It's my turn by the window."
"Shut up!"
"You're hitting me."
"I hate the way you look."
"So do I."
"Are we almost there? I have to vomit."
"I'm sick."
"I have to go to the bathroom."
"I'm hungry, when are we going to eat?"

It was just horrible. I can think about it now and laugh but at the time it was fourteen hours of pure hell. We never learned and we always thought that maybe next year it would work.

One year when we went to North Carolina we decided it would be easier if we drove all night, so we put the kids in their pajamas and packed them in the back of the station wagon. We left about 11:00 p.m. The only problem with this great idea was when they woke up hungry in the middle of the night and we couldn't take them into a restaurant in their night-clothes.

Another year we went to Washington, D.C. because we thought they needed this wonderful educational experience. We took them on a boat ride down the Potomac River, to Jefferson's home, Monticello, and to the Washington zoo. We spent a lot of money because we had to get two adjoining double bedrooms so we could have four double beds—and they never remembered one thing about that trip except for some dumb-looking animal at the zoo. I finally decided that you should wait till the teens when they can understand what's going on.

Although many teenagers and their families find adolescence a difficult time, I don't remember that things were unsettling or terribly unhappy as our children grew up. They had their problems, of course, but our close family life provided a support system for them.

I enjoyed watching our children grow. They were popular and actively involved in school, and they generally did well in their classes. They liked to bring their friends home and I was happy about that. I didn't have to worry about where they were, who they were with, or what they were doing. We had a rule in our house that nobody dated till sixteen, as I did not think that younger teens were mature enough or skilled enough to handle difficult situations.

The girls developed slowly, and sometimes this brought mean teasing from some of their schoolmates. One of my daughters was not her usual sunny self for several days, so one day I asked what was going on. She told me that every day for the past week when she got on the school bus the boys in the back would say, "Here comes No-Tits." I told her, "However you want to handle that, I'll back you up." One particular boy was the ringleader, and she figured if she could handle him the rest would fall in line. The next day after he made the usual disparaging remarks she reported, "Mom, I took my foot, and he was standing up and I just planted my foot right in his chest and kicked him clear down the aisle. The bus driver never said a word to me." The boy said, "I'm going to tell my Mom!" That evening his mother called. She said, "My son has an imprint of your daughter's shoe on his chest." She was angry and threatening. I told her, "Ask your son what he did for my daughter to do that, and what he's been doing for the last week. If you still want to carry this on we'll be glad to meet with you and hear the story from both of them." We never heard another word from the mother.

In addition to our wait-till-sixteen rule and their slow maturation, my children were so busy at school that there was no time for dating. Even the boys were late daters.

Their activities reflected their interests. Anthony was heavily involved with school activities, acting in all the plays and announcing all the games. He normally had the first or second male lead in the plays, and with the many rehearsals I was always driving him there or picking him up.

Allison and Alicia weren't as busy at school as both wanted to work. When Allison turned sixteen she got a job at Strouss, which was then our biggest department store, at the Southern Park Mall branch. When Alicia was old enough she also worked there, and Allan joined them later. He didn't work as much because he was in the high school band, and rehearsals and games demanded a lot of his time. I took him to practice a lot.

Angela and Andrea were also in the band. It was a year-round activity and there were band trips to New York and Washington as well as periodical concerts.

Andrew was busy too. As an auto enthusiast he was usually helping his Uncle Howard work on a car. He was good with engines and also with body work. He was the only one who inherited Tony's fix-it abilities, so he helped a lot with household repairs.

Music has always been important in our family. People who can make music have fun, and I suspect that music helps keep us sane at times. I encouraged the children but never pushed them. When two of them begged to take piano lessons we invested in a used grand, which we discovered later was a magnificent and valuable instrument. In all, there were five who learned to play it. Three later switched to band instruments, but two of them still love piano and take every opportunity to play it.

Our children were not only active and therefore late daters, but they also married later than many young people. Once one of my daughters came home from college and announced that she was getting married.

"No you're not," I replied. She was stunned.

"Why not?" she asked.

"Because you're only a junior, and in this family no one gets married until they have a college education or a profession. Too many things could go wrong, and if you had to support yourself and your children, you couldn't make it financially without an education."

She wasn't too happy at the moment, but later she was glad she had that degree in her pocket. It gave her a sense of security.

Tony's Career Change

Tony loved social work but it had never paid very much. Of course it didn't cost as much to live then either.

Christ Mission shut its doors in 1958 and turned itself into a rehabilitation center something like Goodwill. It did away with the boys' and girls' programs and all of the settlement workers were out of their jobs.

There was no problem for Tony because he immediately went to the Society for the Blind and became a social worker there.

He had always wanted to go into politics. We often talked about that but we knew the timing had to be just right. He decided to run for the Mahoning County Clerk of Courts in 1960. He said, "You know I'm not really crazy about this present counseling job and I have to find something I want to do for the rest of my life. Why not go into politics now?"

This was also the time that he bought the house. When the loan officer at the bank looked at his salary he said, "Tony, there's no way you can afford to buy this house."

Tony replied, "I know that, but I'm contemplating a job change that will pay more money. Just let me ride with this for a year, and if I can't handle it I'll sell it." They decided to go along with it. His proposed change, of course, was politics.

He ran for Clerk of Courts and I was part of his campaign. We were running against a man named William Quinlan who had been Clerk of Courts for twenty-eight years. We also heard that he was a very sick man and thinking of retiring, so Tony decided that this would be THE office to run for.

Quinlan had cancer but the party was trying to keep it quiet. They just hoped that he'd live through the primary, and then if he did die, the party would be allowed to appoint someone of their choosing. That didn't work out because Quinlan died in the middle of the primary campaign.

The party leaders immediately approached Tony and said they would back him.

Tony had originally been a Republican, but in those days they were a very WASPy—party that is, they wanted only White, Anglo-Saxon Protestants with names like Smith or Jones or Brown. When Tony realized he'd never have a future with them he switched to the Democrats.

Some Democrats were behind a man named Za-luski. They denied they were backing him, but many Democratic ballots that we saw passed out had the Zaluski name pasted over the Quinlan name. We knew it was going to be an uphill battle.

Tony won his first primary by three thousand votes—not an overwhelming majority, but comfort-able enough. We did it with hard work: Tony and I, my brother and sister, his family and friends. We had a coalition of people who felt that Tony Vivo was really special. Because we all worked so hard we felt it was our victory too. I was pregnant with Alicia, but I stood on my feet and passed out pamphlets.

His victory was a surprise to the party. From then on I felt he was on his way. He had built such a reputation in the community helping underprivi-leged children, working with the blind and retarded, that people knew he was a beautiful, caring man. He won hands down in the general election against the Republican candidate.

One thing which helped in the general election

was that John F. Kennedy was campaigning for president that year and he came to Youngstown. He and Tony rode together in a convertible as part of a caravan. One thing they had in common was that both Jackie and I were expecting at that time. Jack Kennedy stopped and bought two baskets of apples and told Tony, "You take one to your wife and I'll take one to mine." When Kennedy won, Tony wrote him a congratulatory letter, and he had a letter back from JFK. Tony also attended the inaugural ball that January.

Tony took to politics like a duck to water and I knew it was his field. He had opponents for the next two or three elections, but in the succeeding three elections he didn't even have any opposition. No one tries to take him on now because he built up the reputation of being such a good office holder.

He went in there and turned that office around. The old velvet draperies that hung to the floor in his office were pinned up because they were too long. There was a big hole in the middle of the carpet. Tony cannot tolerate things like this so he got rid of the carpet and the draperies and put in venetian blinds to let the sunshine in.

He adopted new technology as it came along. He went into microfilming and then computers. If there were any complaints about spending money for this he showed the commissioners that all of it was for better service to the public, as indeed it was.

When he first went into office he did something very unusual: he kept all of the original staff. Usually a new office holder replaces the staff, but Tony did not fire one person. This way he had a staff that knew how to operate things and the office continued to run smoothly. Eventually he filled vacancies with his own personnel through natural attrition. The *Youngstown Vindicator* had an editorial on his policy. It said they admired Mr. Vivo for going in and keeping the staff because they knew what was going on and could keep the Clerk's office running. The writer realized that he was a man who walked in without strings because he didn't owe anybody any jobs and he didn't create any.

One of the Clerk's jobs involves naturalization and passports. Tony could see many ways of improving operations there, speeding up the process and making it more efficient. When some of the people from the State Department came in to conduct naturalization hearings and testing they were quite impressed with what he had done. He offered a number of suggestions which were adopted by the Passport and Naturalization Division. The State Department Passport Office honored him by naming him Clerk of the Year in 1972.

Tony's career had taken off. Meanwhile I had also started to crank up my teaching career again.

IV.

Back to Teaching

In 1963 I got a call from the Superintendent's office telling me that my teaching certification would run out unless I got back to the classroom. Since substituting would serve the purpose I decided to become a substitute.

I could do this because I didn't have to worry about baby-sitters. Mother was already in the habit of coming over often to see the children and play with them, to enjoy our home, and to spend time outside in good weather. She and Tony were always interested in the yard. They planted the flowers together and pulled the weeds. I had a vegetable garden and Dad helped out there. They were very much a part of our lives and they often did baby-sitting for us.

When this job opportunity opened up Mother would come over and watch the children the one or two days a week that I normally taught. I paid her and she could use the money, and I could certainly use the income that teaching brought. It was a fine arrangement and went on for several years.

When I first went back I told the principal, "Give me those sweet little first graders. They are really cute." Discovery #1: When you've been away from the classroom for ten years they aren't cute any more. I walked into a classroom and one of those sweet little six-year-olds greeted me with, "You're older than our teacher."

I said, "Sit down, darling. I'm older than everybody."

I still have a scar on my leg from my surgery when I was seventeen. Thirty seconds after I was in the classroom another child said, "Ooh, what is that thing on your leg?" The whole class got up and said, "Look at her leg, it's so gross to look at."

I changed the subject and said, "Children, we're going to salute the flag," and I started to lead them. The children protested and one of them said, "No, no, no, our teacher stands over there to salute the flag." I was thirty-three years old and those children were six—but I ran over to that spot.

At 2:30 they asked, "Are you coming back tomorrow?"

"No," I said, and they all clapped and cheered.

I headed to the principal's office and said, "Don't send me in there any more. They're looking for a Miss America in there. Give me the seventh and eighth graders."

He said, "Mrs. Vivo, are you sure you know what you're talking about? Nobody wants the seventh and eighth grades. We can't give these classes away."

"I want them," I said, and I got them.

It was a Tuesday when I walked into an eighth grade classroom. A young man swaggered up to me and said, "Is this Tuesday?"

I agreed that it was.

He said, "Well, you're just a substitute and you don't know too much, so we're gonna have to tell you a few things."

I said, "Yes?"

"Every Tuesday we have triple period gym," he said. "We have no English, math or history in this school on Tuesday. Then after triple period gym we go out to the playground for the rest of the day. That's what we do in this class on Tuesday."

He turned around to the rest of the class and asked, "Isn't that right?"

They said, "Yeah, that's what we do every Tuesday."

They have great imaginations at that age.

In spite of that questionable beginning we got along well. I loved them and we developed a mutual respect. I never regretted my decision to work with that age group.

Mother

I taught school on Friday, October 13th, 1967. Although Mother was sixty-six she had a great deal of energy, and she had performed her usual small miracles. The house was immaculate, the children were clean, she had baked two pies and had started supper.

She made a point of saying, "Today is Friday. Don't ask me to watch your children tonight because this is my night to play cards." It wasn't really necessary; I knew better than to bother Mother on Friday nights. For years she and some of her deaf friends had spent companionable Friday evenings over cards at the Deaf Club.

She didn't drive, so Dad took her places and picked her up. They went to the car and the children and I went out and waved goodbye to them. As my father backed out of the driveway, Mother gave me the sign which meant "I love you." I gave her another sign back which meant "I really love you." Then they drove down the street.

That night at 12:30 the phone rang. A man said, "Mrs. Vivo, please come down to Southside Hospital. Your mother has just been hit by a car."

I was still dressed except for my bedroom slippers. When I went into the bedroom to get my shoes, I knelt by my bed and prayed, "Oh, God, please don't let my mother suffer or have any pain." I thought that if she had a broken arm she couldn't tell the nurses what was wrong, because of her deafness.

Tony drove me to the hospital. We passed by the scene of the accident, which took place on Market Street just across from the Deaf Club and a block from the hospital. The police cars were there with their sirens still going and Tony pulled over thinking that maybe the man was wrong, that Mother was right there. The policeman said, "The woman's dead, she's d.o.a., she's dead." So that's how I heard about my mother.

Tony said to the policeman, "It was her mother." He answered, "Oh, Ma'am, I'm so sorry. Her body's been taken to Southside Hospital." All we had to do was go around the corner and the hospital was there, and I had just about sixty seconds to cross myself. I wasn't crying, I was in a state of shock, absolutely stunned.

When we got to the hospital the coroner was waiting. He said, "Mrs. Vivo, I'm so sorry. An eighteen-year-old boy was driving the car that hit your mother. From what we can piece of the accident scene her body was thrown very high in the air, probably twenty-five or thirty feet. Because it was hit with such an impact it rolled another twelve feet. Every bone in her body was smashed and broken. She had to have been thrown quite high to be so mangled." Then he added, "The only good thing I can tell you is that she had to have died instantly."

I was devastated, but I knew that I had to collect myself. I had to be in charge, to tell my father, my brother, my two sisters.

I asked if I could see her, but he said no. Someone would have to identify her body but it couldn't be anyone in the immediate family. That just left Tony. It had to be the hardest thing in the world for him, because he had a very special relationship with Mother. When I saw him come out he was sobbing and he said, "Yes, that's my mother-in-law."

Then we called my brother and sister to come to the hospital. When they arrived we all burst into tears, but we knew that we had to compose ourselves enough to go tell Dad. He was sitting at home waiting for Mother. When he saw all of us walk in, he knew that something was very wrong.

We said, "Dad, we have something to tell you. Mother was hit by a car."

He asked, "Is she all right?"

I said, "No, she's dead."

My poor father was crushed. He said, "I wanted to take her to the card club. Every Friday I take her and every Friday I pick her up, right in front. But today she said, "No, no, you always have to take me all the time. You can take me, but the Ruperts will drive me home."

The Ruperts' car was parked across the street, and it was when she walked across to reach the car that she was hit.

Dad said, "I always picked her up in front of the club. She didn't have to cross the street."

Later I realized that everything led up to that day. I

could see that every step she took brought her right to where she was hit. When she started down the steps she said to the Ruperts, "Wait a minute, I want to go back and say something to Ruth McCauley." She went back to her and said, "Your anniversary is next week, and I want to wish you a happy one." Ruth had had a difficult time in her marriage. Mother said, "Just hang in there, things will be all right." Ruth was surprised and said, "You'll be here next Friday night and my anniversary isn't till after that." Mother said, "Well, I just wanted to wish you a Happy Anniversary now."

Mr. and Mrs. Rupert and my mother walked across the street in that order, arms all linked together. When you are deaf and you walk across a dark street at night you always look both ways because you know you cannot hear a car. The Ruperts told us that all three of them looked very carefully as they walked across the street. It was a dark, dreary, rainy night. Visibility was very bad. They all reached the car and Mr. Rupert walked around to the other side to unlock the door. Mrs. Rupert felt a gust of wind, and looked and saw and felt my mother being torn from her grasp and thrown into the air. The car coming across the Market Street bridge evidently was much too close to the parked cars along the street. It must have been that his fender just caught a part of my mother's body. He said he never saw her. Later we would learn that the force of the blow ripped off all her clothes, and she lay naked in the street. When the policeman came, though, he found a black coat covering her nakedness, and no one could figure out whose it was.

A week later there was a call from a priest who had been traveling through. He didn't know if she was Catholic, but he gave her extreme unction and put his coat over her body to cover her. She had just been converted a few months earlier.

After we had talked with Father, we all decided we should call our sister Lee in Houston and tell her that Mother was hit by a car, was holding her own, but that the doctor thought the family should come. We didn't want her traveling on the plane knowing that Mother was dead. Lee said, "But she might die before I get there."

We met her at the Cleveland airport, and as she got off the plane and saw our faces she said, "Mom's dead, isn't she?" We said yes, and all of us had a good cry there at the airport. Then we explained what had happened and told her why we'd lied about it. She understood and said that it was all right, she'd had an inkling that Mother was gone.

Meanwhile, on Saturday morning I gathered the children all together and told them that Grandma had been hit by a car and killed. They all started to cry. They knew that Grandma was in heaven. I told them that she would be with us every day, she'd be walking with us and be with us in spirit. I had mixed emotions about taking them to the funeral home to see her, so I said I didn't want them to go there but they could go to the funeral. I took just the three older ones to the service. I said to them, "I want you to remember Grandma the way she was when she left that Friday night."

I think I made the right decision. They say you should let children know about death. Well, my children know death. They understood that she was hit by a car, she was dead, and they went to the funeral. They saw the finality of death.

My cousin Mary Smith was a hairdresser, and I had asked her if she could do Mother's hair. She loved Mother as much as I did and she said, "My

God, no, I couldn't do that." So we had another hair-dresser do it. When Mary walked in the funeral home before the wake she looked at her and said, "That's not the way Mary liked her hair." She whipped out a comb and re-did it. She said, "I never thought I could do this, but I don't want people to see your mother with her hair done that way. That's not the way she liked it." So Mary did do it after all, and I thought Mother looked beautiful.

The funeral home was jammed with flowers spilling into the next room, which fortunately was vacant. It was a real tribute to Mother because she was so well-liked and well-known, and, of course, Tony was well-known.

Months before her death Mother was teaching sign language to a new priest, Father Henry Lileas, who had been assigned by the Catholic Diocese to work with the deaf. I went to him and said, "I want my mother's funeral mass done in sign language. I think my father has a right to know what is said at her funeral. Besides that there will be many deaf people there, and I think they should also know what is being said."

He replied, "I don't know if I can do it; I was really just learning."

I told him, "I would appreciate it if you would try," and he said he would.

I'll never forget how Father Lileas did that. He had the microphone on but he was also signing. He started out by using the wrong sign, then said, "No, I want to start over again." He did, and he did so well. My father could understand everything, and even those who weren't deaf cried through the whole thing because they had never seen a funeral so meaningful and beautiful.

One line in it I will never forget. I have used it and I've passed it on to others because it was so helpful.

He said, "You know, we all loved Mary so much. Even I loved her and I've only known her a few months. She was so warm and loving and charming, and she didn't have a mean streak in her. She was so special. But Mary is gone, so let's take all the love we have for her and give it to somebody else who needs it."

Mother's will was lovely. She had said, "I want to leave my wedding ring to my daughter Leona because she is the only one who has ever admired it," and that was true. I had never looked at her wedding ring as something that pretty, but Lee always did. She'd say, "Mom, I love your ring, it's so beautiful."

Mother left her china to me because we had the two homes together and we always shared things. She had specific and thoughtful bequests to each of the children, and we were so moved.

She also left all of her clothing to me to pass on to her deaf friends. Mother had a tendency to be a little plump, so I knew the women who were to have her clothes. They were all very poor. Mother had a closet full of lovely clothes, and I made several trips to Akron to distribute them.

Dad

My poor father not only lost his wife but he lost the only person with whom he could communicate intimately. My brother Leo had never married and he still lived at home, but it wasn't the same. Dad was completely devastated and I watched him die a little every day.

Two months after her death the house beside us was put up for sale. I talked with Leo about it and said, "Why don't you look at this house? It's just perfect—there are two bedrooms—and I think Dad should get out of the old house. There are too many painful memories." He could not understand why his wife had been taken from him. He questioned it all the time. He'd walk around saying, "Why isn't my wife here with me? Why isn't she in bed with me? Every time I look in the kitchen I think I'm going to see her there." He was not hallucinating, he was trying to grasp why it all happened.

Leo and Dad looked at the house and liked it, and Dad was tickled pink to think that he'd be next door to his grandchildren.

He sold the old family home and the move was the best thing that could have happened to him. He started to fail quickly, and this way I could care for him.

Before the move Dad was grieving and brooding a lot. He said, "The boy who killed her never even wrote to apologize." This ate away at him, so Tony pressured the detective working on the case to have him write. A week later the letter came.

"Mr. Gilboy," it said, "I'm so sorry I killed your wife. I didn't mean to. I didn't see her. It's something I'll have to live with for the rest of my life."

At the accident the boy was screaming hysterically, looking at her body. "Please say she's alive, please say I didn't kill her."

He was a suspected drug user, but they didn't have the tests then and he got off scot free. He said he was going twenty miles per hour in terrible weather conditions—rain and fog—and they couldn't prove anything.

The letter seemed to soothe Dad's sense of justice, though nothing could stop his grief.

After the move I was over there three and four times a day. Sometimes he'd stumble and fall and I'd find him. I finally had to take the car away from him because the police picked him up for going the wrong way on the freeway.

His driving skills had diminished as he got older. When he was younger I always felt very safe with him, but that changed. When the police stopped him that night and brought him to the station he was furious. He wrote notes to them: "Do you know who my son-in-law is? He's Tony Vivo, Mahoning County Clerk of Courts. He's a very influential man and he'll have all your jobs."

The police called us and Tony went down immediately. He could have died when the officers said, "Look at what your father-in-law wrote, Tony. He's going to have all our jobs!" They were more amused than annoyed, and gave Tony the notes.

The next day we went to look at the ramps, and they were quite confusing. The exit and entrance were right next to each other and it would be easy to make a mistake at night. It was fortunate that he was picked up before he did any damage. He could have killed other people as well as himself.

He had a bad case of arteriosclerosis, hardening of the arteries. All he did was watch TV, and he'd walk around and play with the children.

One day I found him wedged in between the toilet and the wall, and he couldn't get up. I knew then he couldn't stay there alone all day, so we moved him to our house in January, 1972. I remember that it was very cold, and my husband and brother carried him. He was nearly seventy-six at the time.

Anthony, who was thirteen, said, "You can move him in my bedroom." I was so proud of him. We got a hospital bed for Father and put it in Anthony's room, and he never got out of bed after that. I set my alarm every two hours and turned him, so he never had bed sores.

Kay Welsh, a nurse across the street, taught me how to take care of him. She'd be over every day or so and give him a bath for me. He had wonderful care. The doctor wanted to put him in the hospital, but I thought he would die a more dignified death at home. At the hospital he'd have tubes coming out of him, and I didn't want that. I knew the time was very close.

I woke up on Thursday, March 17th, and he was so bad I knew he wouldn't last the day. I made sure that my brother and sister were both there. Kay also came in. She told me, "When he dies, put his dentures in his mouth immediately so his mouth does not set. Otherwise he won't look real at the funeral home."

At 6:00 o'clock I told the children, "You know, Grampa is very close to death. I think you should all go in and say goodbye to him." So they went in and took his hand.

He'd always had a cookie or candy for the kids. He'd say, "Look in my back pocket, I've got something for you." The kids would cock their heads: "Grandpa's coming. I wonder what he has?"

I told the children, "Why don't you go in and eat supper, and I'll sit with him. They did, and at 7:00 he drew his last breath. Dot, Leo and I were with him.

I went to the kitchen to call the funeral home, and the children went in for one last goodbye. It was my sister Dot's birthday and she asked, "Why did he have to die today?" I prayed, "Oh God, let me say something that will help her." I found myself saying, "Hey, Dot, listen to this: of all the days Daddy could have died, he chose your birthday. March 17th will always be special for two things—it's your birthday, and the day that Daddy chose to die." She looked at me and said, "You know, I never thought of that." I was so grateful to be able to say something to her.

It was a privilege to take care of him, and that he never had to go to a nursing home.

We called my sister Lee and she flew in for the funeral. It was a lovely one and it was also in sign language.

V.

Professional Speaker

The spring after Mother died I got a call one day from Sister Maureen, a friend of mine who taught in a Catholic school. She asked me to have lunch with her. She inquired about the children and I told her some of the crazy things they'd been doing. She found it all very hilarious and laughed her way through the lunch hour. It was a pleasant Tuesday afternoon.

On Thursday I got another call from her and she said, "Our speaker on marriage can't come Saturday evening. Can you take her place?" This was for a group of teenage girls.

I said, "Are you crazy, Sister? I've never given a talk in my life."

"Just say what you told me at lunch," she replied. "Talk about your kids, your family, your marriage, for an hour. They'll love it."

"One *hour*?" I groaned. "I can't talk that long."

There was no getting out of it, so painfully and reluctantly I began preparing little note cards. After I'd jotted down everything I could think of I hoped it would last an hour. If it didn't, too bad, because I didn't have any more. Then I lined up the children to serve as a practice audience and I asked ten-year-old Anthony to time me.

When it was all over he said, "Seven minutes."

Seven minutes? Well, it couldn't be helped.

When I arrived at the retreat center I said to Sister Maureen, "You'll just have to tell them that since I only got the request on Thursday there wasn't time to prepare a full speech. Tell them I'll talk for seven minutes and then take questions." When she introduced me she ignored my instructions.

She said, "Wait till you hear this next speaker. You're going to love her and she's going to talk to you for an hour."

There were fifty girls seated casually on the floor. They were wearing jeans and sports shirts or sweaters. There was a clock in the back of the room and as Sister Maureen introduced me it pointed exactly to 5:00 o'clock. I said silently, "God, please get me through the next hour."

I started going through my notes and as I came to the first topic I remembered something similar which had happened in our own family, and I told that story. The next topic triggered another memory, and the next one still another. I ended up telling about the death of my mother. "I could accept her death," I said, "because I had told her many times that I loved her. I didn't have a lot of unfinished business. People don't know we love them unless we tell them. We can't plan to wait till later to tell them because we really don't know that they'll be there. We have to tell them now."

When I finished the last line I looked up at the clock and it was exactly 6:00. The girls were all on their feet crying and they headed out to the hall telephone, where they lined up to call their parents and tell them they loved them. My own mother's legacy had moved them.

The priest and the two nuns there said, "We've never seen a reaction like this to any speaker," and they asked me to keep coming back to these retreats. During the winter months they ran two of them each week for high school seniors from Catholic schools throughout the diocese. The final evening they would end with a talk on marriage and the family. They had both boys and girls but never together, and the students came from all kinds of backgrounds.

After that first talk I felt as though God had written right on the wall, "Pat, this is what I want you to do for the rest of your life." I was so happy working with these teenagers, I was completely hooked. I felt fulfilled.

One week some of the boys were really roughnecks—in fact, the priest described them as hoodlums. As I was introduced some of them started to act up, but then their leader said, "Shut up! I wanna hear this broad." They all got quiet and I said to this young man, "Thank you." I spoke to them just as I did to everyone else, and their response was beautiful: a loving, caring reaction. Of course, while I was talking I was also praying for them as well as for myself.

Over the years I spoke to more than six thousand teens in groups of fifty. Although some of the stories changed from time to time the message was always the same, yet I was surprised at how it always seemed so fresh to me. I told them, "It's wonderful to have a child when you are married and want one; it's not wonderful when you are single." I told them what it was like to have a big family, and took plenty of illustrations from the seven children I had in eight and a half years. Most importantly I told them, "We've got to love each other, and we've got to tell others that we love them because they're not mind readers. They won't know unless we tell them and show them."

There was a real rapport with this age group. I learned that many teenagers are hurting, unloved and uncared for, and it seemed that my story was one they wanted and needed. After my talk they would come up to me and tell their stories. Sometimes one or two of them would take me off in a corner of the room so they could talk privately. Most of their questions were about sex, and in the 1960s some of their questions knocked me for a loop. They were sexually active and asked things that were totally outside my range of experience.

The first time I got such questions I looked at the girl and said, "I'm shocked by what I'm hearing, but I'm glad you're telling me because I think you ought to talk to someone. I can't relate to anything you're saying because none of these things were demanded by anyone I was dating. I think emotionally you're going to be the loser. Women get wrapped up in a relationship much more than men do. You are so filled with love right now and you think this is the man you're going to marry, but he probably isn't. What you want in a man at sixteen or seventeen is not what you'll be looking for at twenty-one or twenty-two. I believe you should tread very carefully and think twice about the things you are doing right now. I think you are headed for heartbreak because you are not ready for this kind of deep commitment socially, sexually or psychologically."

One day when I was secure in the belief that this was my life's work, the church decided not to have the program any more. I was devastated, empty, almost grief-stricken. Part of this was because I knew I'd really been able to help these young people and now that channel was closed. Part of it was because I had learned so much from them. But there was another reason.

Over the past few years I had found a beautiful, creative way to express myself. I had never been a musician or an artist, but being chopped off from my speaking experiences was as painful as a musician suddenly without an instrument, or an artist without a canvas. I had developed all this skill and there was no way to use it. There was little wonder that I was depressed about it.

Then one day a few weeks after it ended I had a call from a young married woman. She had been in one of the retreats years earlier and had been impressed with my message. Now she was in a club and had been asked to get a speaker, and she wanted to know if I were available. I said that I was.

"Oh—and what are your charges?" she asked.

Charges? I was unprepared for that question. Did people actually get *paid* for doing something they love? I thought quickly and said, "Ten dollars."

"Oh, we can handle that," she said. "Our last speaker charged $25, and he was terrible."

Needless to say, my fees went up the next time I was asked.

As word of mouth spread I began to get more and more requests to speak. Gradually I built up a local reputation, and just as gradually my fees increased.

One evening early in 1979 Tony and I went to dinner where they had a wonderful humorist, Joe Griffith. He was hilarious and I simply howled at his stories, and so did everyone else. After his speech I stood in line to meet him so I could tell him what a great speaker he was.

He was very friendly and said, "You really made me look good."

Then I said to him timidly, "I'm a speaker too."

"Are you serious?" he asked, and I assured him that I was.

"Then you should be in the National Speakers Association," he said. He went on to explain that it was an organization of professional speakers. It would give me an opportunity to get to know others in the same field, and there would also be a great deal of practical help in developing a brochure and marketing myself and my message.

It sounded good to me so I decided to join. They had a national convention every July as well as regional winter workshops.

I wanted to go to that 1979 convention but there just wasn't enough money. I called my sister Lee and asked her, "How would you like to subsidize my first NSA convention?"—and I told her all about it. She never hesitated for a moment but just asked "How much?"—and wrote a check for it. To this day she has never let me repay her.

Not long after the convention I got a card from Dr. Trudy Knox announcing that she was going to start the Ohio Speakers Forum, and she invited me to become a charter member. I joined that year but because of commitments I couldn't get to the meetings for two years.

I never missed an NSA convention after that, and they were all that Joe Griffith had promised. That year and in 1980 and 1981, my older children who were working each gave me $100 to help with expenses. After that I was making enough to go on my own.

At the 1981 NSA convention a couple of very prominent Ohio speakers mentioned how much they got out of the OSF meetings. I thought, if they get so much out of it even though they are successful, then maybe I ought to make time to attend. I did so, and from the first meeting found OSF to be invaluable. They met in Columbus approximately every other month, and from that first meeting I worked my engagements around it. It was there that I met Barbara Yoder Hall, who became one of my closest friends.

Early in my OSF years I was on my first showcase, which is an event where speakers give brief presentations to meeting planners and program chairs who are looking for speakers. I gave a summary of my speech on "Turn Right at the Next Corner," which is based on the stories in this book. When I finished a gentleman came up to me and introduced himself. He said, "I'd like to use you for a number of Safety Council banquets over a three-year period." He offered me more for one speech than I had ever dreamed a speaker could make. I tried hard to look calm as I said I could do that for him.

Also through the Ohio Speakers Forum I met a fellow professional speaker by the name of Mike Frank, who owns one of the most successful speakers' bureaus in the country. After the showcase he came up to me and said, "I'm very impressed with your speaking ability. Please send me your brochure and a tape." He added me to his list of speakers, and many times he would recommend me if someone called him and asked for a speaker on family life, communication, motivation or humor.

In addition I had a few other single offers from the showcase, so that one experience put me on the road to real professionalism.

Sometimes people get upset when they learn about a speaker's fees. But when you stop to think about it they aren't getting as much as it sounds. Even if you are giving the same one or two speeches all over, there is still preparation time for each group. Some speakers spend twenty hours or more preparing for every speech. There is also travel time. The client pays travel expenses, but if you have to spend several hours tied up in getting to airports and back, or waiting for connecting flights, or driving, all that has to be added to your total cost per hour.

Marketing costs also have to be figured in. This includes the cost of brochures, cards, stationery and postage, not to mention phone bills. These are things I hadn't even thought of earlier, but they made the difference between being a professional and an amateur. When I began it was a hobby, but now it is a full time job.

From the high school retreats and then local clubs and organizations, I moved to after-dinner speeches, opening or "keynote" speeches, and closing speeches for conferences and conventions, school assemblies, teachers' in-service days, and commencements. Most of the commencements were for high schools, but there were a few colleges and junior colleges. There my subject was "What Are You Going to Do with the Rest of Your Life?"

I developed several different topics for different groups. For mother-daughter banquets it was "Hello Mother, Hello Daughter," and if fathers were present that was changed to "Hello Parents, Hello Children." Today I average over a hundred speeches a year. Most of them are still in Ohio, but increasingly I am traveling throughout the country.

Someone once asked how my children reacted to my speaking. As they have grown up they've had a better appreciation of what I do, but respect was not always automatic. Once I was in a bit of a preaching mood, which can sometimes be an occupational hazard. I was speaking with a then teenage son about a whole parcel of problems: "We need to talk about. . . ." "While we are on the subject, I think you ought to. . . ." "You ought to think about. . . ." "And another thing. . . ." He had just about had it and he said, "You mean people pay to hear you talk?" He slammed a ten-dollar bill on the counter and said, "Here's $10. How long will you shut up for this?"

I was mad and I said, "Take it back—I want to talk to you!" Later I thought it was a marvelously funny line and I've used it many times.

My Professional Family

After about three years of regular attendance at the Ohio Speakers Forum I was asked to be on the Board of Directors for the 1984–85 year. The next year I was elected second vice president, where several committee chairpersons reported to me, including ethics, long-range planning and publicity. Following that I served for two years as first vice president with a number of other committees under my umbrella, such as education, networking and the showcase.

By the time I became president in 1988 I had learned the behind-the-scenes operations. In addition to being responsible for the committees, I had taken on a number of other small jobs such as welcoming new members, giving them OSF materials, and whatever else needed to be done. As president I would make sure that OSF had directions and goals for the year, pick qualified and capable people, and learn to delegate work. The theme which I chose for the year was "Speaking Is Our Business and the Keyword is Professional."

I was deeply moved that my speaking colleagues wanted me to serve as their leader for two years, and I could accept this only because so many of them were willing to help. In the years that I have been in OSF I have discovered the members to be beautiful, caring people, and I look forward to attending every meeting. I always learn something worthwhile, and I am constantly meeting new and interesting people.

War Stories

Every speaker has experiences where things don't run smoothly, where the equipment doesn't work properly, or any of a hundred other things can go wrong. We call these "war stories," and often trade such stories when we get together.

Most of my war stories were embarrassing when they happened but when I thought about them later they were funny, so I've often used them in my speeches. They've brought so many laughs that now I've learned to use them immediately and turn them around to my advantage.

Introductions are often a bit scary. I always send an introduction and I take a couple of copies with me, but you never know what people will do with them.

Once I was speaking to a group of five hundred men, ranging in age from sixty-seven to nearly a hundred. The man who was to introduce me had lost the first two copies I sent him, so I gave him a third, and this is what he said: "If Mrs. Vivo doesn't talk too long today maybe we can have fun afterwards and play cards."

Another time I was speaking to a nice-sized group of women. When the president introduced me she followed by saying, "I'm so embarrassed we have such a small crowd for Mrs. Vivo tonight. I can't understand why we have so few. We publicized widely that Mrs. Vivo would be our speaker. The only other time we had a small crowd like this was four years ago and we didn't have a speaker that night." I didn't know it was small until she said that, and it certainly didn't do much for my self esteem.

I gave fifty-two Safety Council speeches across the state of Ohio for the Division of Safety and Hygiene. After my introduction in Piqua a man stood up and said, "I don't know what the heck a mother of eight is going to tell us about safety." That brought a good laugh and I thought, I'm going to use this, which I did in my opening sentences.

It always amazes me how people can mangle such a short, simple name as Vivo, which should be pronounced VEEvo. I have been introduced as VIVE-o, Video, and other variations. One of the funniest ones came when the program chairman said he had known me for five years, that he was privileged to present me, and then introduced me as Pat Vivelo!

There are often interesting conversations before the speech. Once I spoke to the Rotary Club in Cleveland, which, I understand, is one of the largest in the world. I sat beside a very nice gentleman who asked, "Are you going to be our speaker today?"

I said that I was.

He said, "I've been a member of Rotary for many, many years, and we've never had a woman speaker before."

"Oh?" I said.

He asked, "What does your husband do?"

"He's the Mahoning County Clerk of Courts," I replied.

"Oh, is he a Democrat?" asked the Rotarian.

"Yes," I answered.

"And are you?"

"Yes."

Then he hesitated and looked me right in the eye and said, "We've never had a Democrat speak to us before, either!"

It was a pleasure to widen their horizons. After my initial reaction I thought it was funny, and I've used it many times.

A few years ago I substituted for Woody Hayes at a couple of commencements when the feisty Ohio State football coach had a heart attack and had to cancel. The principal and two of his board members had heard me speak shortly before that and they decided to use me in his place.

I was standing in the hallway before the ceremony began at the first one, and I overheard the groans of some of the men present who had learned that a woman was speaking in his place. It's an uncomfortable feeling to hear people talking about you in that way.

When I started to speak I said, "I know what all of you men did on your way to this commencement. You turned to your wives and said, 'You mean I'm not going to hear Woody Hayes today, that a *woman* is replacing him?' But I have a right to be here. First of all I just put my fourth child into Ohio State this fall, and second, one of my daughters is dating one of his former football players." After the speech several of the men came up and complimented me, and one of them suggested that I take up coaching, too!

Being a woman speaker has some hazards attached. In the beginning I got lots of phone calls like this: "Mrs. Vivo, we'd be interested in having you speak to our group but we've never had a woman before. What do you charge?" When I'd tell them they'd say, "Well, we paid a man that much last year and I don't think this group will go for paying a woman the same amount."

One time when that happened I said, "Sir, are you implying that I should speak for less because I am a woman?"

He said, "I just don't think the men will go for this."

I answered, "I'm sorry, but I'm just as good as any man you've ever had and I'm not charging less."

"I'll get back to the board and I'll talk to you later," he replied.

"Fine," I said. "You tell them that I'm going to be the best speaker they ever had." Why I said that I don't know, it just slipped right off the end of my tongue.

He called back a week later and said that the board had agreed to have me at my price, and then he added, "There was only one negative vote."

"Oh?" I asked.

"Yes," he said, "It was mine."

I said "Thank you for being so honest. I'm looking forward to meeting you!"

Speaking to children also has its risks. Once I was addressing a large group of fourth graders, who were seated around the floor so they could fit more of them into the room. I was especially struck by one little fellow who was giving me his full attention. After I made a few points I looked right at him and asked what he was thinking.

"I can see right up your dress," he replied.

Whenever you get to thinking you're very special someone brings you right down. If it isn't a child, it's an adult.

I do a lot of speaking for the Ohio Child Conservation League and I go back to some of their groups two or three years in a row. I was in my third year at one of them and was so pleased that they wanted me to keep coming back. I walked in and a woman said, "You must be the speaker."

"Why?" I asked. "Do I look like a speaker?"

She said, "No, you wore that same dress last year."

If she remembered it others would too, so I seized the initiative in my opening line. I said, "I really do have another dress—I know you don't believe it, but I do. It's green, and I will wear it here the next time I come."

Some speakers keep very careful records of what they wear at each engagement, just to make sure this sort of thing doesn't happen. I've never been quite that well organized, but I'm about to start.

Sometimes your clothes can betray you. Once I had a brand new gray cotton dress which I decided to wear to an engagement with a large school system in Ohio. I was going to be there two days, the first day speaking to the classified staff of eight hundred and the second day to the teaching staff of nine hundred.

I arrived in town the night before and unpacked, and I noticed that my new dress needed pressing. I got out my iron and went over it, and spots started coming out. The more I pressed the worse they got. I put some water on the dress and sort of rubbed them out, but then when I pressed the water spots the others came out all over again. Did you ever see a grown woman cry? It was 11:30 at night and I had to go on at 8:00 the next morning, and there was definitely no time to go buy another dress. I was in a motel in a strange city and there were no friends to call on in the emergency.

Perhaps when it dried it would look better. I got up in the morning and it was a little fainter, but the spots were still noticeable. I thought I might be able to press it then, and the spots came out strong again. I am sitting there talking to myself, asking me how I could be so stupid.

The spots were all on the back of the dress. I put it on and went gamely in. When something like this happens you might as well acknowledge it immediately and then get on to business.

After the introduction I said, "You may forget my name, you may never remember my speech, but don't ever forget that I'm the speaker that had the spots on her new dress and she couldn't get them out." I turned around and showed them and went through the whole story and they all got a laugh out of it.

The second day I went back to talk to the other group and they said, "You're the one with the spots on the dress—turn around." I did, and they said, "Oh yes, there they are!"

A couple of times I've forgotten a slip. When that has happened I've just said, "If you can see through my dress you should, because I forgot my slip. So please try not to look except from the waist up."

At least I don't have to worry about runs in my stockings. I've learned to carry extras with me at all times.

Every speaker has nightmares about arriving late, or worse yet, missing an engagement.

Once I was to speak in Beverly, Ohio, a small town some two-and-a-half hours southeast of Columbus. I was running late and I stepped up my speed on Interstate 70. I was looking out for the Highway Patrol, watching ahead, on the sides and through the rear view mirror. As I turned a bend there were some patrol cars with their lights flashing. I slowed down and drove past, but a woman officer waved me over gently and nicely.

I said, "What's the trouble, Ma'am? Do I have a broken headlight or something?"

"No," she said. "You were clocked going 72 miles an hour."

"I don't understand," I replied. "Where were you?"

She pointed her finger up in the air and said, "You were clocked by one of our radar planes." She motioned for me to get in her car.

It had been a long time since I'd had a ticket and I was sick about it, especially since I was late. I asked, "How will I pay for it?"

She asked, "Do you have a Visa or Master Card?"

"Yes," I replied, and pulled out the plastic.

"Then you can pay it now," she said, and reached for her little credit card machine.

When I got my Visa card and license back I started once again, and now I was really late. I had to step on the gas, but this time I opened up my sun roof and glanced furtively up there as well as in the front, back, and on the sides.

When I got to Beverly I headed for the school, where several hundred people were waiting for me at a regional Ohio Child Conservation League meeting.

I made it just on time as they were sitting down to lunch. I sat beside a woman and said, "I just got a ticket for speeding."

She said, "Oh? My daughter's a State Highway Patrol officer."

"Really?" I said. "What does your daughter look like?"

"She's very little and has light brown hair," said my companion.

"That sounds like the officer who picked me up," I observed. I reached for my Visa slip to check the name, but there wasn't any name.

"They just use their badge numbers," she said.

The number 416 leaped out at me. "That's my daughter's badge number," she noted. Then I learned that her name was Charlene and I had the impression she was an officer, I think the president.

When I got up to speak I told them the whole story, and the incredible coincidence that the officer was Charlene's daughter. They started to howl, then I had a sudden inspiration. I turned to my new friend and said, "And Charlene's going to get me my money back." Charlene's mouth dropped and she kept shaking her head as the laughter went on.

Whenever I go to a strange community I have to have very explicit instructions. I have a terrible sense of direction and if you tell me to turn east or south, you'll lose me. I need something like, "Turn right at the Sohio gas station and then left where there's a big red church." I've often found myself driving around a town completely lost, with everything closed up and no one to ask directions. I'd often drive on a country road while telling myself, "You are going in the wrong direction." One time I was not even aware I was going the wrong way until I came to a huge sign which said, "You Are Now Entering Pennsylvania." Since my engagement was in Ohio I turned around and pulled into the first gas station to ask for help. The attendant said, "Lady, you are *really* lost."

One time a principal told me to take 39 East when he meant 39 West. I didn't bother to check it on the map, which was a great mistake. By the time I discovered the problem I was an hour and a half away, and I was supposed to start talking in fifteen minutes. I barreled back there as well as I could, and arrived to find the principal and his wife standing outside looking for my car. He groaned when he heard about the wrong instructions but it worked out all right. They had coffee and cookies while they were waiting.

Now I ask my clients for very definite directions that are lost-proof.

One time when I didn't do that because I thought I knew the territory so well, I got into trouble because everything had changed. I was to speak at the Akron Civic Theatre, and because one of my daughters went to the University of Akron a few years earlier, I didn't ask for instructions. Unbeknownst to me the whole city had changed. Some streets had disappeared, others had been added, and still others were one-way streets. When I finally drove past the theatre, people were lined up outside waiting for graduation. I thought, I'm the speaker and I'm not even there yet. By then there was no parking and I had to go some distance to find a parking lot that still had empty spaces.

If I am ill—and that has happened just once—I make arrangements in advance. The only talk I ever missed came because of transportation difficulties.

I don't like flying to speeches because of delays, problems with connecting flights, and other potential trouble.

I had a speech scheduled in Dover, Delaware, on one day and Warren, Ohio, the next day. There certainly shouldn't have been any problems. I flew in to Philadelphia and then rented a car and drove to Dover for my talk. I got up at 3:00 a.m. the next day and drove to the Philadelphia airport in plenty of time for the 7:00 o'clock flight to Pittsburgh. I walked up to the clerk and said, "I'm ready to get on my Pittsburgh flight."

She replied, "Nothing's flying into Pittsburgh this morning. It's all fogged in."

"You don't understand," I said. "I have to fly to Pittsburgh—I have a speech at noon."

"*You* don't understand," she returned. "*Nothing* is flying into Pittsburgh."

I couldn't believe it. I asked when they thought the fog would lift.

"I don't know but we're hoping by 8:00," she said.

I called Tony and said, "There's a strong possibility I may not make my talk. You'd better call the nuns at the school system and tell them that I'll do my best but I can't guarantee anything." Warren is near Youngstown and Tony could reach the sisters easily.

There were over a dozen calls to Tony in the next few hours before I finally realized there was no way to make it.

The next day I called the Sister in charge and apologized. She said, "We're definitely going to have you next year," but I never heard from her again. Missing a talk can be hazardous to your career.

If my speech is within six to eight hours from home, I prefer to drive, where I feel I have more control over the situation. When driving is impossible I try to go early enough to allow for any problems. Unfortunately there isn't much you can do about fog.

Certified Speaking Professional

About 1985 I began thinking that I'd like to get my CSP, the NSA designation for Certified Speaking Professional. There are many requirements for this and since my record keeping left something to be desired, I wasn't sure I could meet them all. In the winter of 1988 I felt very strongly that if I didn't do it then I wouldn't do it at all. There had to be 250 speeches within the past five years, and they had to have paid a certain amount. I had plenty of speeches, but they didn't all meet the minimum payment required. There had to be at least one hundred different clients, twenty testimonial letters, and every single talk had to be verified.

There were record sheets from NSA which had to be filled out. There were five lines of information for each speech, and five sets per page. They wanted to know for each engagement, the date, title, client name, address and phone; hotel or other location of the speech with name, address and phone; the fee charged, and whether this was a repeat client.

My sister Dot and I talked about it, and she said, "Let's go through all your records and find out how many talks you have." She came into my office and she was appalled at the state of my records. She asked, "How are we ever going to find anything in all this?"

She had to go home, so she said, "Put together everything you can find and I'll see what I can do." I started going through all my cabinet doors, along with drawers, nooks and crannies in my office and bedroom, and started finding all kinds of things. This included every letter I had, every thank you, every contact and every program. I threw them all into boxes and a couple of days later I took them over to her house.

Dot said, "What am I supposed to do with these?"

"The first thing is to categorize all of them," I replied. "We'll have to separate them by year from 1979 on. Then we'll have to take those years, separate them into months so we have some idea of how many talks I do have."

Then I went away for three days of speaking, and when I returned I couldn't believe what she had done. She had taken all those scraps of paper, envelopes, letters and programs and somehow made some sense out of the whole mess. They were all in envelopes where they belonged, and they could be easily checked. Dot said, "I loved doing it. It gave me something to do, and I wasn't bored."

Our next job was to find out what we were missing. We took the NSA sheets and I ran all the necessary extra copies so we could save the good ones for the final typing. We started filling in and discovered we were missing so much information. We might have the name of the client but no address or phone, or the name of the hotel but not its location. We filled out what we did have, and that took hours and hours, with Dot doing most of it.

Then we had to start calling information to get numbers. Luckily I have two phones at home, one is mine and there's another for the family. Even though most of my children had left I kept the number because it was on all my brochures. She used one phone and I used the other, and we just started down the list. We'd call the operator and ask for the number of X hotel in Y city, get the number, then call the hotel for their exact address. If we had the name of the client and the city we got the information and then called her. My sister posed as my secretary because I was too embarrassed to have her say, "This is Pat's sister," so she said, "This is Pat Vivo's secretary and she is applying for a designation in NSA. She needs information about this speech, and unfortunately she has lost it."

Through this monumental amount of phone calls—I wish you could have seen my phone bills the next month—we finally started filling in the holes. It was really crazy because we couldn't get hold of a couple of people even with lots of calling. I remember specifically one woman in a little town in southern Ohio. I tried morning, noon and night and wondered why she wasn't answering her phone. Finally I called the public library because I knew it was a small town. I said to the librarian, "I'm looking for X," and she said, "She's my neighbor and she's in Florida. I think she will be back Monday or Tuesday." I asked her to have X call me on her return, and she promised to do so. Sure enough, a few days later she called me and we had a good laugh over it. I got all the information I needed from her.

When we finally got it all we had fifty-three pages of five talks listed on each page with all the information. Then we needed someone to type it, and as you can imagine this is the hardest kind of thing to type. It wasn't like a letter; we're talking names, addresses, zip codes and phone numbers.

My sister's daughter Cheryl is a wonderful person and a highly skilled typist. I asked her, "Do you think you could type this? It is quite difficult." By the time we had all the information we had only a week before the deadline, so I was really placing her under a great strain.

"Oh, I can do it," she said. After she started and did two or three pages she realized this would be very difficult. She started typing it on her lunch hour, coming in early before work and staying two or three hours after work to get this done. I will be grateful forever to my niece and my sister. When I got the designation I wanted to shout out while I was on the stage, my sister and my niece ought to be standing here because they're as much responsible for my getting this award as I am.

It was a wonderful moment. There were twenty-five people given the award that year, only four of them women. That made me one of a total of thirty women in the country with the CSP that year and only the second woman in Ohio. I'm proud of this because I worked hard as a full-time professional. Now when I see CSP after others' names I respect them because I know what they've done to get these letters. And I'm deeply indebted to Dot and Cheryl for all those long, tedious hours to help me become Pat Vivo, CSP.

VI.

Moving On

When it came time for college most of my children opted to go to schools far enough away that nobody would know them as one of the Vivo kids. Ohio State was the most popular, but Ohio University at Athens attracted one. They majored in education, hearing and speech therapy, audiology, business, communications, industrial hygiene, nursing, film and video.

When one of my daughters had been accepted and enrolled in Ohio State and was ready to start her classes in September, in the middle of August she came into my room and said, "Mother, when I lean my neck back I can feel a lump." She showed me and I did feel a lump on her neck, so I called the doctor and we went over there that afternoon. He looked at it and said, "I really think we should have this X-rayed." So we went to the lab and the doctor there said, "I think you should have a surgeon look at this."

So we took her to our surgeon and he said, "I can aspirate this in the office—no problem." He tried to aspirate it, which is removing the fluid with a needle, and he couldn't do it. He said, "I'll have to remove this surgically. But don't worry, I do about twenty-five or thirty of these a year and most of them are benign." We scheduled her for surgery and it had to be very soon because of school starting. We got her in right away and we asked how long the surgery would take. They said about an hour and a half.

When she was in surgery two, two and a half, three hours, I said to Tony, "Something is terribly wrong."

Every hospital waiting room has a chapel, so I went into this one and prayed, "God, whatever it is, just let me be able to handle it."

About a half hour later the waiting room phone rang and the receptionist picked it up. She told us, "The doctor wants to see you in the hallway by the surgery door." We went out and the doctor whipped through the swinging doors. He still had on his surgical gown and cap. He pulled off his cap and said to us, "We were shocked when we opened her up. Your daughter has papillary carcinoma of the thyroid."

I looked at him and said, "How does an eighteen-year-old girl get cancer cells in the thyroid?"

"I don't know," he replied, "but you're going to have to make some decisions because there's a controversial treatment about cancer of the thyroid."

In the next few days he gave us the names of five doctors scattered across the country, all of whom specialized in papillary carcinoma of the thyroid. When the doctor and my husband and I went in to tell her that she did indeed have cancer, we thought she took it very well. Oh, she cried after the doctor left, but I still thought she was very brave.

After she got out of the hospital we made the rounds of the doctors who'd been recommended. As we were coming out of Sloan Kettering in New York City we had a couple of hours before our plane left, and we were walking along and stopped at a street corner in the city. I turned and looked at her and she said, "Mom, I have cancer. Help me." We clung and held on to each other on that street corner in the heart of New York City. I said to her, "Darling, we are helping you. We are getting the best medical care available in this country and we are going to lick this."

The bottom line was, we went with the radioactive iodine treatment which was supervised by a specialist from Ann Arbor, Michigan, and done at our own local hospital. Then she took herself off to Ohio State.

The next few months were difficult for her because of the rudeness of some people who would look at her and say, "How come you have that scar on your neck?" She was sensitive about it, but she would say, "I had an operation," or, "It's really none of your business," or sometimes she would just look at them and say nothing.

She had to have a body scan every year to make sure the cancer had not spread throughout her body. She is now in her twenties and doing quite well. I'm proud of her. It changed her personality just a little bit—but why wouldn't it? It's a major thing in your life to have cancer.

When she saw the movie, *Terms of Endearment*, I remember how much it upset her, and how we talked about that. She said, "But Mom, the girl died." I said, "I know it, but she didn't have the same kind of cancer you had." I thank God today for allowing me to get through this and be supportive of her. I had terrible nightmares that she wouldn't make it. She is very near and dear and special to me.

One of the things which helped us get through this difficult time was the support of friends. The night we found out she had cancer, while we were sitting in the waiting room, Tony's secretary came and spent the evening with us. When she left she went downstairs and called our good friends Stanley and Joy Malkoff and told them, "You should see these two people. Pat and Tony are devastated. They love you so much, do you think you could come down and sit with them a while?" Sure enough, about 11:00 or 11:30 Stanley and Joy walked into the hospital and stayed with us until about 2:00 in the morning. I'll never forget Stanley saying, "Whatever you have to do, if you have to take her anywhere, fly her anywhere, if you have to incur any expenses, I'll pay for it." I will never forget that.

Tony's Accident

In March of 1985, Tony was in a terrible accident. He was driving home a new car and he braked to a stop when he came to the stop sign on the small side street. Dusk was turning into darkness and the cars all had their lights on. He looked both ways, saw that it was clear, and pulled out onto the main highway.

At that moment a car without lights came over the hill, and hit him broadside on the driver's side with such force that he flew out of the car and landed across the street in the middle of the road. Luckily no traffic was coming or he would surely have been killed. He had a broken ankle, lacerations on his elbow, a slight concussion, lost three or four teeth, and had abrasions all over his body.

The woman who hit him had been drinking and she never even stopped for two or three blocks. People were waving and motioning to her and she finally came to a halt and asked, "Did I hit someone?"

Of course the one thing which ran through my mind was, "I'm going to lose my husband like I lost my mother," but fortunately that was not the case. The first night in the hospital it was clear that he would make it. He was in for eleven days, and he was pretty well healed within two months and able to go back to work.

As Tony regained his strength he gradually resumed most of his activities, and life returned to normal.

We have a real appreciation of such groups as Mothers Against Drunk Driving, MADD, and the youth organization which came out of it, Students Against Drunk Driving, SADD. They are doing a wonderful job of educating people to realize that drinking and driving don't mix. There is still a great deal to be done, however.

School Board

Because of my concern over the education of the deaf, for years I had in the back of my mind that I would like to be on the Mahoning County School Board. I was interested in that rather than our local Boardman School Board because only the county had the responsibility for deaf education. Besides that, I was completely satisfied with the work of the local board and didn't see that I would make that much difference on it.

While my children were young and still at home I simply did not have the time. Then when a friend who shared my philosophy was appointed as Supervisor of Special Education, that dissolved a major reason for running.

As the children left home I thought increasingly of the board. There had never been a woman on it and the time seemed right to try for it. The only thing that held me back was that I had the highest respect for the five men on it, and I hesitated to run against them. Two of them had been on for twenty years and I heard rumors that they were getting ready to retire. That did not occur, however, so I took stock of the situation and decided to run. I certainly had the qualifications. With experience as both a parent and a teacher I could see two sides of educational issues and make some contributions.

Board members serve four-year terms with elections every other year. Two members run one year and the other three, two years later. That would insure that there were always experienced members.

In 1985 the three men were running, an attorney and a dentist who had both been on twenty years, and a retired Superintendent of Schools with eight years behind him.

My first job was to create a campaign committee of twenty people, which included my husband Tony, who was our advisor; my brother Leo, the treasurer; and eighteen of my women friends. We met weekly throughout the entire campaign, mostly at my home. Since we had a low budget we had to do a lot more footwork. We knocked on doors, had coffee klatches, passed out literature at football games, and more. We collected hundreds of signatures of people who wanted to see my name on the ballot, then we had to go to the Board of Elections and check every name to make sure they were all legal and would not be thrown out. Only one name was questionable.

The daughter of a committee member had a boy friend who was a graphic artist. He did our art work and designed a logo: a stack of books with an apple on the top and the words, "Pat Vivo, A New Direction." Actually the kids were planning to break up, but we persuaded them to wait till after the campaign! The logo appeared on brochures, T-shirts and flyers. We advertised in football programs but could afford only one or two small newspaper ads. In contrast my three opponents pooled their funds and ran a very large newspaper ad.

One effective thing we did was to take out a booth at the Boardman Oktoberfest, which draws some 55,000 people. My son Andrew designed and built a frame to run our banner high over the table. There we shook hands and passed out hundreds of apples daily.

All of our efforts paid off on election day. There were five people running for the three seats, and voters checked off three names. When the results came in I had the top number of votes, with the dentist and the attorney following.

Three things helped me win: First, the fact that I was married to Tony Vivo who was a highly respected politician; second, my professional speaking had brought me to nearly every women's group and high school in the county, so I was well known; and finally, but not least, that wonderful, hard-working committee that believed in me.

The board members accepted me fully and were kind and helpful in explaining things. The former superintendent, who was now off the board, was especially gracious. He told me, "I couldn't have been beaten by a nicer person."

Being on the board automatically got me also on the Mahoning County Joint Vocational School Board, a wonderful, eye-opening experience. It is unique, with a special and caring staff dedicated to the students. The students want things that the home school cannot provide. The home school might have a business program with shorthand and typing, but not all the business machines or the data they will need to get jobs. All of the JVS programs have the high technology needed for the workplace.

Each board meets monthly, and I work my speaking engagements around the meetings. I believe I have made a difference, and others have confirmed this. Among other things there is less sexism. In the beginning when anyone wanted to present something to the board the introduction was always, "Gentlemen," because that's always the way it was before. Now they acknowledge that I am no gentleman as they reach for more neutral terms. I have loved being on the board and was re-elected in 1989 to a second four-year term.

Homecoming

Most of the children have left home now as they have gone out to their careers or to marriage or to both. A few still live in the Youngstown or Columbus areas, but others have moved farther afield.

On holidays the whole family comes to our house because we have the most room, with our kitchen table seating eighteen to twenty. My sister Dot comes with her husband, daughter and son-in-law; my

brother Leo; the married children and their spouses;
all of the children who are close enough to make it;
and my college children and any friends they want to
bring home. Sometimes we have other friends there
as well.

When we sit down to dinner I begin with a prayer,
but I do it differently every year. Sometimes I'll have
them all hold hands. Or I say a couple of things that
I'm feeling and then pray. One year we were around
the room and they all said how they felt about getting together for holidays. One of my sons said how
proud he was to be a member of this family. A
daughter said, "I thought all families did this till I
went away to college. Very few people do what we
do, and I love my family for it." It was moving to hear
each one.

If someone isn't there we always have a prayer for
that person, and if we've been through some bad
times we ask for help in getting through them. When
we found out that our daughter had cancer it
knocked the whole family for a loop. There were lots
of tears shed, but we all drew in tighter together. We
surrounded and supported her and told her we loved
her, and that gave strength to all of us.

Our holiday homecomings are joyous times. We
laugh and have fun and kiss and hug when they
have to leave. We are even closer now than when the
children were small, because we have all grown together.

Of course we are also in touch between holidays. If
I am speaking in a city where any of them live, I am
in contact with them and perhaps stay with them.

Since my brother Leo lives next door I see him almost daily, and I see my sister Dot quite frequently.
We have had some wonderful nostalgic sessions talk-

ing about our childhood while I was working on this book. It was interesting how many things they remembered that I had forgotten.

Leo remembered growing up with the deaf. When he got out of high school in 1951 he worked for Ohio Edison for a while and then spent two years in the armed forces and was stationed in Germany. Mom regularly baked cookies and sent them to him all the time he was gone. On the night he returned she did not want to go to the airport to meet him, as it was dark and she wouldn't have been able to see him signing in the car. So she baby sat while the rest of us went.

After his return he started working at the *Youngstown Vindicator* in the composing room, where he still works today. He has the opportunity to help some of the deaf employees there and is happy to do it.

Dot remembered Mother making the curtains for her windows when she was first married. She also made lovely baby clothes when her daughter was born, and later they were passed on to my daughters.

Lee is separated from us by the miles, but we are in touch, and she too had a share in the book.

We recalled our entry into the adult world. As we grew up and started working we all helped our parents. While Leo was working at Ohio Edison he bought them a washer and dryer at the employee's discount. He also got them a chandelier for the dining room, and every so often he would bring in $50 or $60 worth of groceries. I bought the living room furniture and the lamps, and I bought most of Mom's dresses.

Our stories have moved from past to present and back again, but underlying everything is an appreciation of growing up with such wonderful people.

VII.

Barbara

In our backgrounds Barbara Yoder Hall and I were about as opposite as you could get. She was born in the strictest Amish sect, the sixth of eleven children. Her early years were spent in their simple lifestyle in Holmes County, Ohio. There was no electricity or indoor plumbing or telephone, and their transportation was by horse and buggy. Their clothing was severely plain.

When she was eleven her parents decided to leave the Amish faith, and since it would have been difficult to remain in their old home, they moved to Hartville, Ohio. Although her family was "in the world" then, they were still quite conservative by most American standards.

After her marriage Barbara told one of her neighbors stories of her Amish background. Later the neighbor asked Barbara to speak to her club, and her speaking career developed from that. Then her audiences wanted to know her better, so she wrote *Born Amish*, a series of tales of her Amish childhood.

Lyle Crist, an OSF member who was a writer and college professor, had been a mentor to her while she was writing her book. He brought her to the Ohio

Speakers Forum and pointed me out to her, and she came up to me during a break. She said, "I'm Barbara Hall and Lyle Crist says I should hook up with you if I want to know what speaking is all about."

She had a very friendly, pretty face, and I liked her immediately. We hit it off at once, and soon after she called me and asked if she could come over and bring a tape of her speech for my critique. I said, "Certainly!" and about a month later she came with a couple of tapes. We played them and I told her very frankly what needed to be changed. She took criticism so well; she soaked it up like a sponge. I think that was her strongest point. She'd say, "You're right. I never noticed that before." She did everything that I suggested and it worked. I was trying to save her some of the pitfalls that I'd had in my early years of speaking.

One day I said to her, "Barbara, you have to throw away your notes." She said, "I don't know if I can do it without the notes."

I said, "Sure you can." About a week later she called me and said, "Guess what! I did a talk today without my notes and I was very good!" I said, "Of course you were!"

The next thing I told her was, "Barb, you've got to get away from that lectern. Come out from behind it and walk around."

She said, "I couldn't do that." She was a somewhat heavy woman who was self-conscious about her size, and I think she thought it was more secure to stay behind the lectern.

I said, "No, come out in front. You always look nice and you dress nicely; let them see you."

A month later she said, "I did it! I got from behind the lectern and I walked all around, and it was wonderful! I felt so free. You were right."

Sometimes when people ask for help what they really want you to do is tell them how good they are. If you tell them they need to change they will disappear and that's the end of that. But Barbara was serious about wanting to improve and she took advice from anyone she trusted who knew what they were doing. I think that's why she got so much better in speaking so much faster than the rest of us did.

We became strong and fast friends over the next few years. We decided to go to the Ohio Speakers Forum together, with the meetings in Columbus every other month. It was a little out of my way but it was nice having company for the trip and I didn't mind it. It took me forty-five minutes to get to her house and then about two and a half hours to Columbus. Of course, the camaraderie and the conversation were wonderful. We talked all the way there and all the way back, and there were thousands of things to talk about.

The friendlier we got, the more we discovered we had in common in spite of our seeming differences. I had eight children, she had four. We both had the same philosophy about marriage and motherhood. We were concerned about our children and wanted them to be happy. We both had the same kind of husband: men who supported our speaking careers but who didn't quite understand what speaking was all about. We kept finding more similarities in our lives.

We always went to Columbus the night before the meeting because I had a board meeting then. We shared the cost of a hotel room and it benefitted both of us.

Then we moved on to doing the NSA conventions together, taking the same plane and sharing a room there. I introduced her to many of my old friends, and she introduced me to new friends she'd just made.

I have had many good friends in my lifetime and they have been precious to me, but Barbara was my first speaking friend, the first who could share my professional life. Not many people know what it's like to be on the road, what it's like to get in front of people, what it's like to bomb in front of a crowd, to be exhilarated when you get a standing ovation. Barbara was my first friend whom I could call and say, "Guess what happened today. . . ." and she'd say, "Yes, that happened to me last month."

She also clung to me. She would say to me, "I'm going to be where you are in a few years. I'm going to charge as much as you do, dress like you do, have a car like yours." She felt she could grow with me in the speaking profession.

She had had a lifelong dream of opening an Amish restaurant. She found a man who was willing to invest in it and she opened her Amish restaurant in Middlefield, Ohio, naming it after her mother—Mary Yoder's Amish Kitchen.

My sister and I went up on opening day. It was a lovely restaurant and she was so proud of it, but she had to spend eighteen to twenty-two hours a day there, sometimes sleeping in the office at night. She had so much to do.

Dot and I went up a couple more times over the next few weeks, including just a couple of days before Christmas. I had ordered a dozen of their wonderful Amish pies, and my sister wanted a couple. We sat there and had dinner and talked with Barbara, and she gave each of us a gift, a box of Amish greeting cards. We hugged each other and wished each other Merry Christmas, and out the door we went.

That was the last time I would see Barbara alive. On the night of January 13th—actually 2:30 a.m. on the 14th—the phone rang. It was Ed Hall, Barbara's husband, and he said, "Pat, we've lost Barbara. She was in an automobile accident tonight and was killed."

I don't remember what I said the next few minutes. I do remember that he had to hang up because he had to make a lot of other calls. So about twenty minutes later when I'd pulled myself together I called him back for the details.

She was not supposed to come home from the restaurant that night, but was to stay at the office as she often did. She decided to go home because her sister was there from Oregon, and Barbara was going to take her back to the restaurant the next day. She was coming down a rural road which was not too heavily traveled at that time of night. It was slippery in parts and evidently she hit an icy spot, swerved into the next lane and an oncoming car hit her directly on her car door, killing her instantly.

When Ed gave me all those details I hung up the phone again and went into the family room. It was after 3:00, and I just sat there in the dark until about 7:30. I was thinking, I've lost a best friend, and I've never lost a best friend before. I've lost a mother and father and relatives, aunt and uncle, but I have never lost a best friend. I'm never going to see Barbara Hall again.

At 7:30 I picked up the phone and started calling her speaking friends all across the country. Of course, their reaction was just like mine: they were shocked, there were tears, they couldn't believe it. I probably made about thirty-five phone calls that morning.

Her funeral must have been the largest that the town of Hartville ever had; when the cars in the funeral procession reached 125 I stopped counting. I don't think Barbara ever realized the impact she had on people's lives.

The funeral service was quite unusual; I'd never been to one quite like it. After the pastor sang a song he said, "I'm going to sit down and anyone who has anything to say about Barbara, please feel free to get up and do so."

There was silence for a couple of minutes and it felt like ten minutes, but the pastor still sat there calmly. Then the wife of the restaurant owner stood up, her grandchild nestled on her shoulder, and said, "Barbara was a very loving person, and we shall miss her very much." Then pretty soon another woman stood up and said, "I belong to Barbara's church and I'll never forget how many times she helped me." Then someone else got up and said, "She was so good to me; I don't know what I'll ever do without her." On and on it went all over the church.

Then I heard Barbara's voice inside my head saying, "You mean to tell me, Pat Vivo, you are not going to stand up here and say anything nice about me?" I thought, of course I have to, so I stood up. For the first time in my professional speaking life I was scared to death, for I wanted to say the right thing. So I said, "On behalf of all her professional speaking friends I want to tell you how much she gave to the speaking profession, and how as a woman she elevated it for all women. I want especially to speak to the Amish people in this room, because she gave the public out there such an understanding of being Amish. Everyone who left her talks had a warm, wonderful feeling for all of the Amish people." I don't remember what else I said, I just remember my heart beating very loudly and I sat down. But I didn't hear the voice any more so I knew that was what she wanted me to say.

Afterward her sisters came up and said, "We cannot tell you how much that needed to be said, because so many people in the Amish community resented Barbara going out and being so worldly, and they needed to know how much she had done for them."

After a few months, a good friend told me that I was still not over the grieving process. Maybe I wasn't. I remember going over to Barbara's house one evening and spending time with her husband and three of her sons. It is difficult for all of them, but it is also difficult for me. I know she's with me; I feel her with me so many times. Often I go to the phone to call her and tell her what has happened, then I say, "No, Pat, you can't do that."

When you have a good friend whom you can trust and to whom you can say anything and know it will never go any further, you are rich. I was so enriched by Barbara Yoder Hall. She gave me so very much.

VIII.

My Extended Family

As my speaking career developed I began to get more and more requests to speak to teenagers, and every time I spoke to them I heard their stories. Some were on drugs or alcohol. Some wanted to commit suicide. Others were victims of adult sexual abuse. They all had a terrible problem with self image, and many of them just wanted to talk. They said that no one would listen to them.

I was especially haunted by one beautiful young girl. Her hair came down to her shoulders, and she was so sad. She said that her mother often told her she was no good. In the name of God, how can any parent tell a child a thing like that?

A boy confided that he'd had a big fight with his mother the day she died in an automobile crash. He felt he would have to carry that with him the rest of his life. I told him, "Mothers are the most forgiving people in the world, and I know she has already forgiven you. But I'll tell you something you can do: you can reach out to someone who is lonely and doesn't fit in, and draw that person out." When people share their love and concern it helps build self esteem in others. It says to them, "You're valuable."

116

Many who didn't stop to talk wrote letters. One said, "You gave me hope for a better tomorrow. I was one of those kids you talked about who didn't fit in. No one ever reached out to me—or at least I never knew if they did—and I put up a wall so no one could get close to me. That is, until I heard you speak. I realized I wasn't the only one to go through all that. This time, for the rest of the week I let the girls in my group get close to me, and because of that I'm a better person."

Another wrote, "As you started talking about your mother and her death I thought of my grandmother who is in the hospital. If she would have died before I could say 'I love you,' I would have felt so terrible. I went back home and I told her that even if she couldn't say it back to me I knew she did by her eyes, and then I took her hand in mine. I wanted her to get better and live with us, and then I realized that I wanted her to live for me and my selfish ways. I felt so terrible. I said to God, 'Either let her live pain free or be with you and Grandfather in heaven.'" Last Wednesday I stopped in again to tell her that I love her, and that evening she died. I miss her so much, but I know how happy she is."

Many had been so scarred by their families and their pain was still so great that they could not release it. One young girl wrote, "I hear you but I don't believe you. I can't, you see. I can't love. . . . I hate." Once when I spoke at a high school, during the question and answer period a young woman stood up at the back of the room and said, "Mrs. Vivo, I loved your talk, but don't tell me about parents. I'm eighteen years old and I can't remember once my mother ever touching me or holding me or ever saying she loved me. And I can't remember my father ever doing anything but calling me four-letter words." Then she began to cry.

A few were not in pain, but seeing it in others around them they were able to appreciate their own circumstances. One wrote, "Fortunately I have a very open and respectful relationship with my family members; you made me appreciate that even more. Thank you."

Another wrote, "My fellow Girls Staters and I stayed up most of that night talking about things that many of us hadn't even discussed with ourselves."

Not just teenagers but adults have also opened up their hearts. Many times after my talks a woman will come up to me, hold my hand, look me straight in the eye—most of the time with tears in her eyes—and say something like, "I wasn't supposed to come tonight but my boss's wife couldn't make it and I was asked to come in her place." Or, "The couple that was supposed to come couldn't attend, so my husband came home an hour ago and said, 'Come on, we're going to a dinner.' I didn't want to go, but here I am, and now I know I was supposed to be here. I can't tell you how you touched my life, or how I needed to hear the things you said tonight."

Or perhaps one may look me straight in the eye and just hold so tightly to my hand. She may go no further than that before leaving, or she may go into a story.

A woman wrote, "You said we should forgive our parents and love them. At this point I can't. I hope by the grace of God at some later time I can. I'm not so sure all parents try their best. . . . Nobody can hurt you like a parent can, and for some reason a lot of parents think they have a license to do so." Another confided, "I had been told from a little girl I was stupid. I only went to the eighth grade, so I knew I was stupid." With this belief she questioned everything she did, and only later realized that she had done her best and had instinctively done what was right for her.

I am a family woman, and it was growing up in a loving family, then having my own wonderful family, which showed me that there is no shortage of love. When you love someone it doesn't take away from your love for another, but you just have that much more to give. Because of that loving background I have been able to reach out to my audiences, who have truly become my extended family. They are special people to me. As my speaking career escalates each year I realize there are many more special people out there just waiting for me as much as I am waiting for them.

There is room in my heart and memories for all of them.

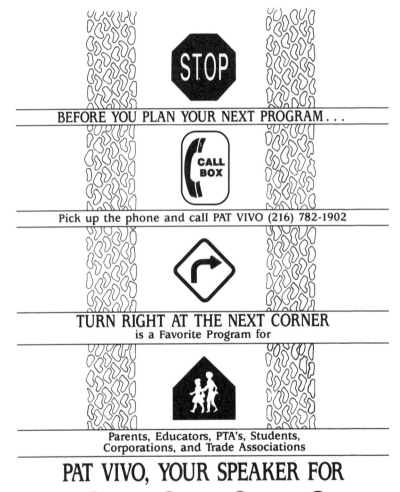

BEFORE YOU PLAN YOUR NEXT PROGRAM...

Pick up the phone and call PAT VIVO (216) 782-1902

TURN RIGHT AT THE NEXT CORNER
is a Favorite Program for

Parents, Educators, PTA's, Students,
Corporations, and Trade Associations

PAT VIVO, YOUR SPEAKER FOR

| COMMENCEMENT | KEYNOTE | AFTER DINNER | CONFERENCE |

PAT VIVO   743 Nellbert Lane   Youngstown, OH 44512

ORDER BLANK

ATTENTION: SCHOOLS AND CORPORATIONS

Trudy Knox Publisher books are available at quantity discounts of over 50 books, with bulk purchase for educational, business, or sales promotional use. For information, please write to Special Sales Department, Trudy Knox Publisher, 168 Wildwood Drive, Granville, OH 43023-1073, or phone 614-587-3400.

MAIL ORDER TO:
TRUDY KNOX—PUBLISHER
168 WILDWOOD DRIVE
GRANVILLE, OH 43023-1073

Total

Please send _____ copies of the book, *Turn Right at the Next Corner* @ **$7.50** $_____books

Add for postage, $1.50 for one or two books, .50 for each additional. Please add additional for delivery outside the United States. $_____postage

OHIO residents, add 6% sales tax $_____Ohio tax

ENCLOSED IS CHECK OR MONEY ORDER
          U. S. FUNDS ONLY $_____Total
Payable to:
Trudy Knox—Publisher

SEND TO:

NAME _____

                                        APT.#
ADDRESS _____ SUITE # _____
CITY _____ STATE _____
PHONE ( ) _____ ZIP _____
PLEASE ALLOW 4-6 WEEKS DELIVERY